Anti-Stress
Colouring
doodle & dream

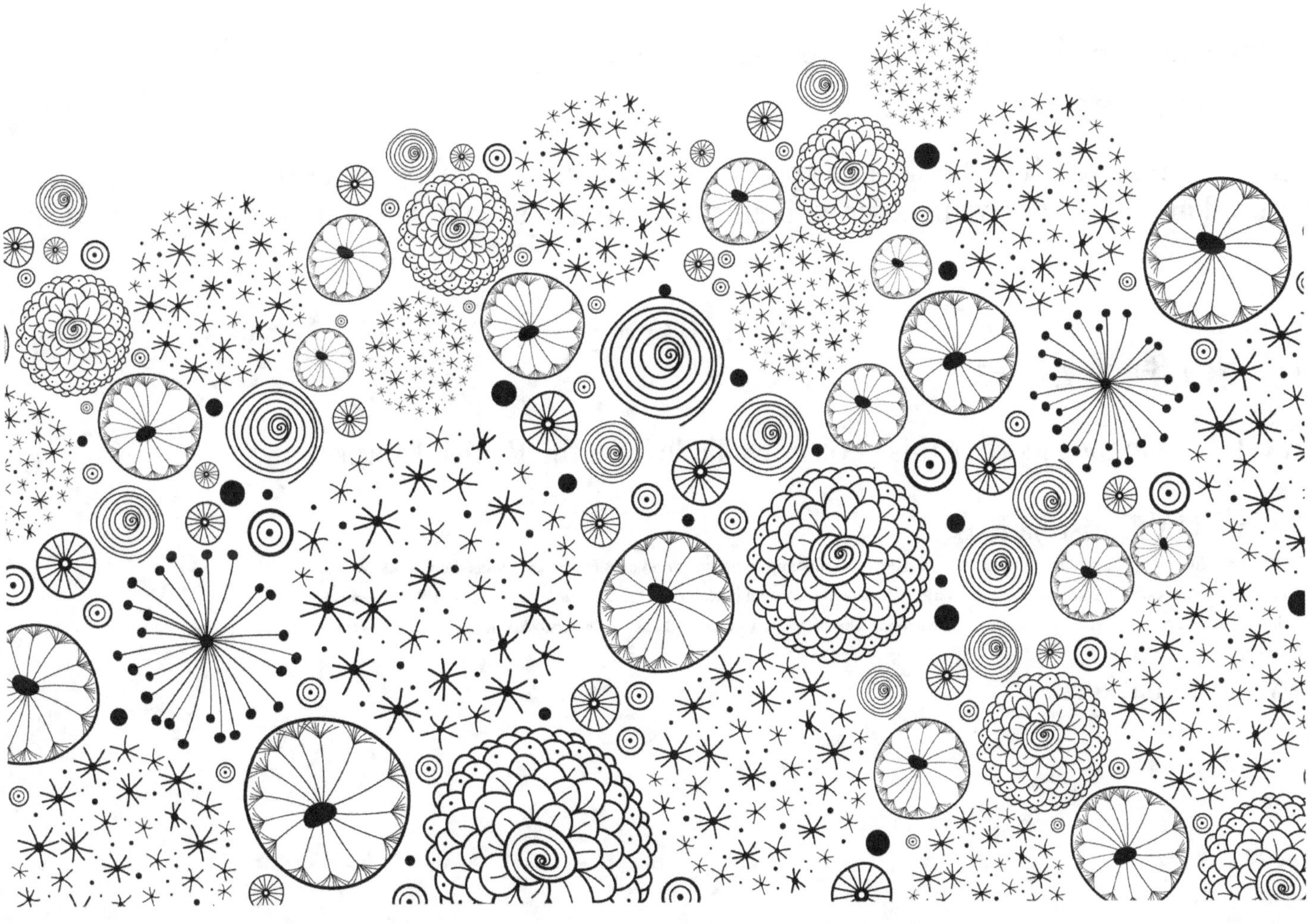

Anti-Stress Colouring: doodle & dream

First published in the United Kingdom in 2015 by
Bell & Mackenzie Publishing Limited

ISBN: 978-1-910771-16-7

A CIP catalogue record of this book is available from the British Library

Created by Christina Rose

Contributors: Julia Snegireva/shutterstock, julia badeeva/shutterstock, hoverfly/shutterstock, An Vino/shutterstock, Liukas/shutterstock, Maria Zvonkova/shutterstock, Sablegear/shutterstock, Maria Zvonkova/shutterstock, Emila/shutterstock, maralova/shutterstock, Naticka/shutterstock, Melissa King/shutterstock, abdrashitova svetlana/shutterstock, Sadovnikova Olga/shutterstock, Tanor/shutterstock, karakotsya/shutterstock, SkyLynx/shutterstock, zabavina/shutterstock

www.bellmackenzie.com

This book belongs to

Being in control of your life and having realistic expectations about your day-to-day challenges are the keys to stress management.

Marilu Henner

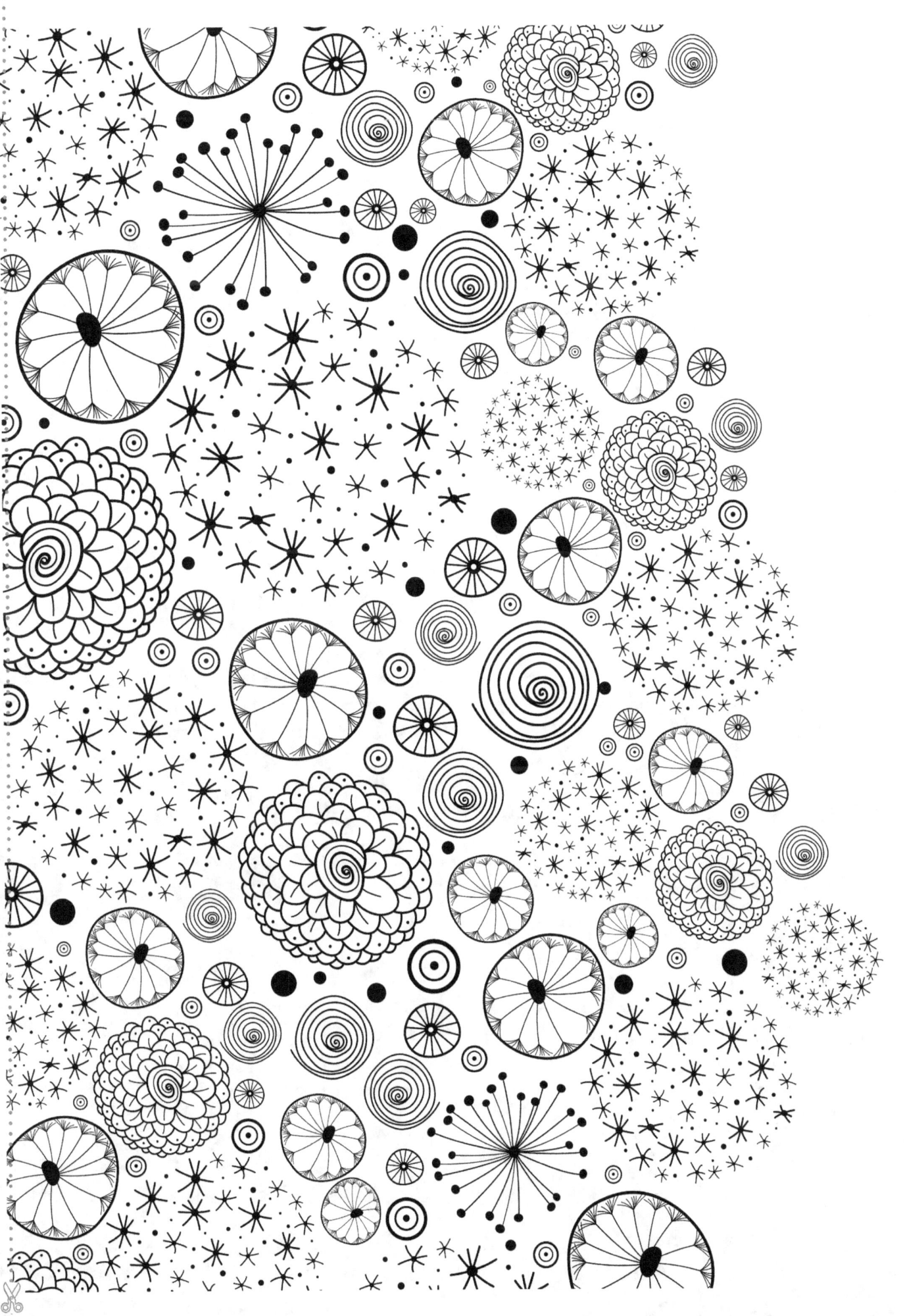

There's a lot of stress out there, and to handle it, you just need to believe in yourself; always go back to the person that you know you are, and don't let anybody tell you any different.

McKayla Maroney

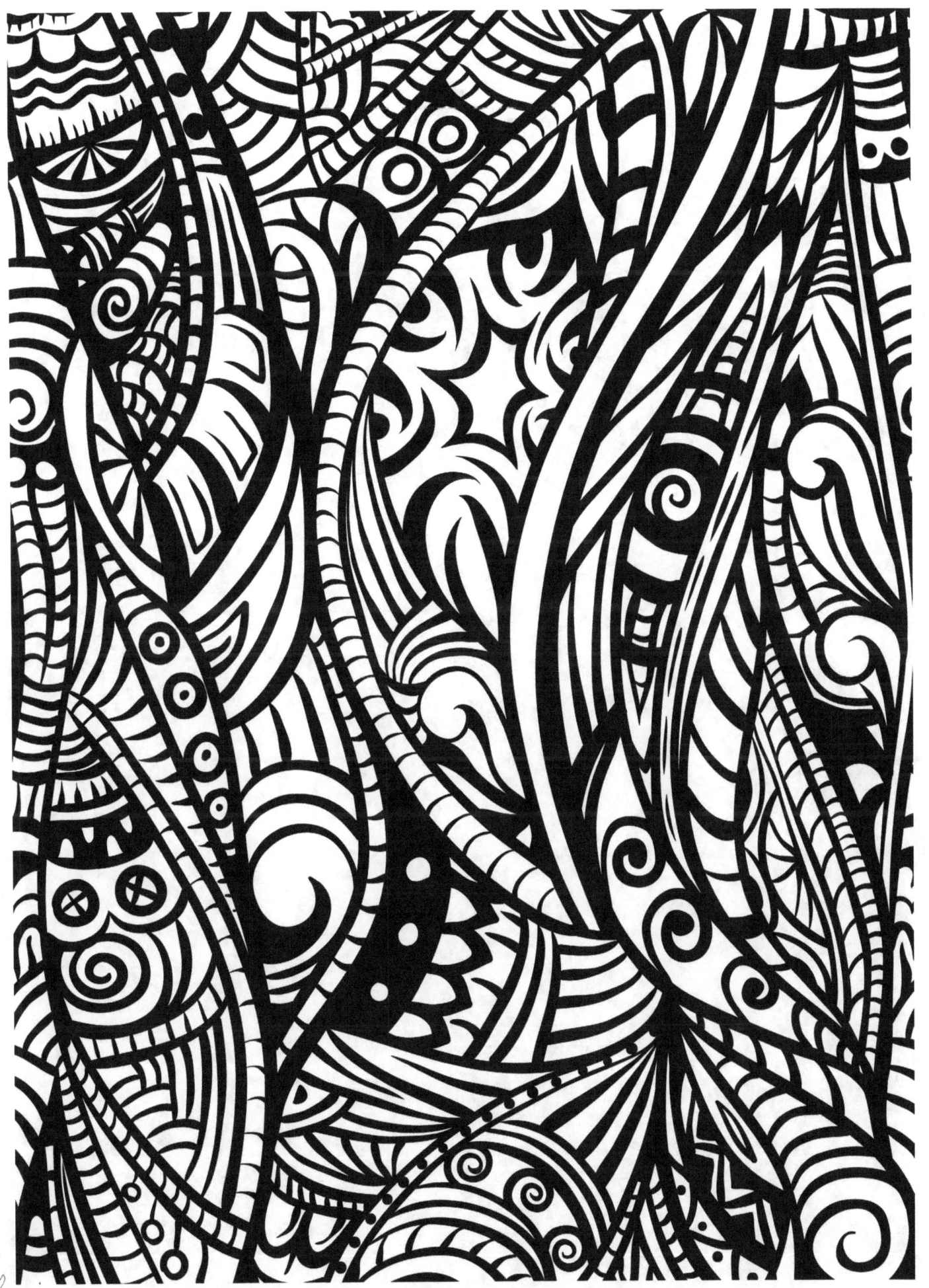

If you don't think your anxiety, depression, sadness and stress impact your physical health, think again.

Kris Carr

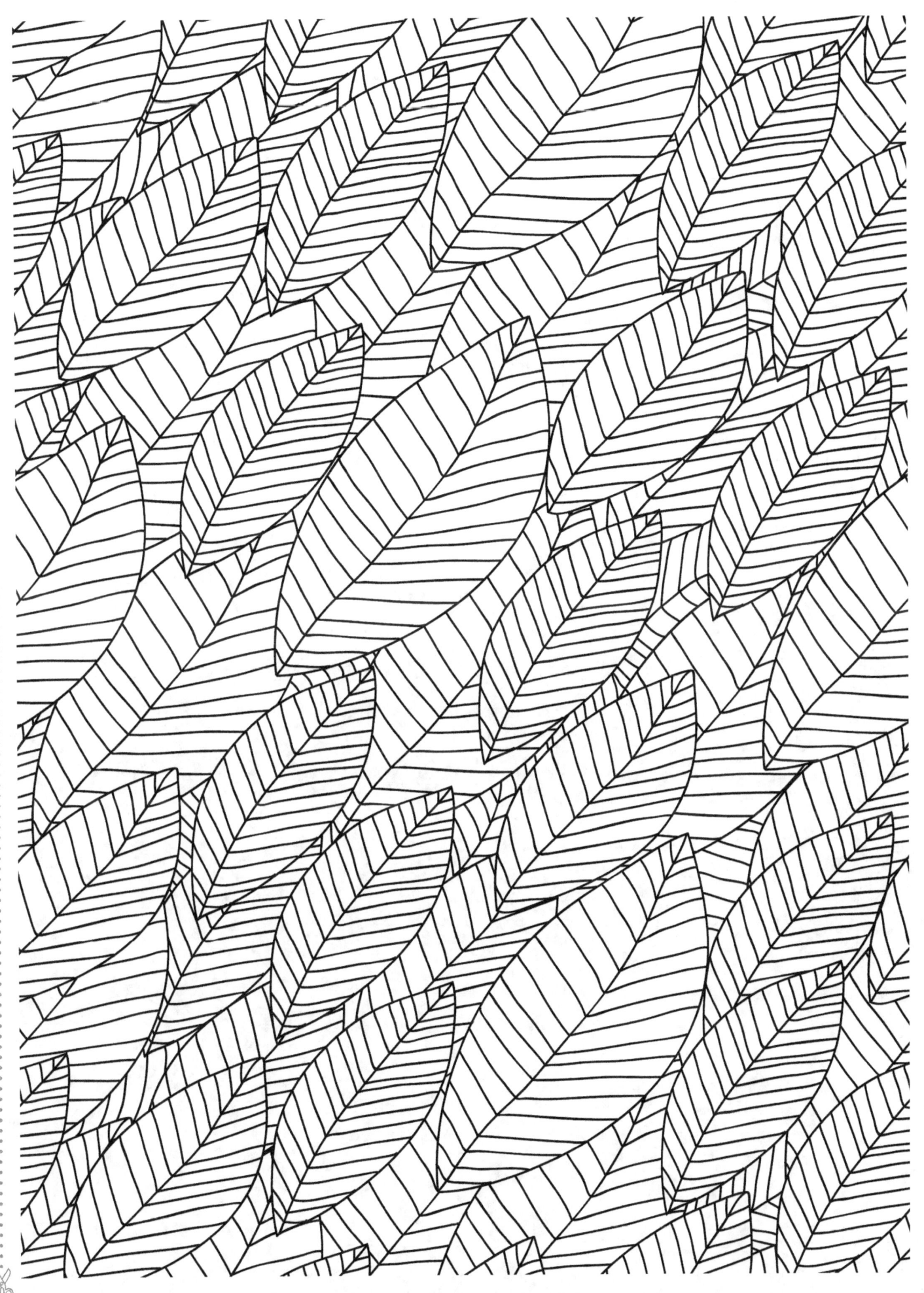

Happiness is a choice. You can choose to be happy. There's going to be stress in life, but it's your choice whether you let it affect you or not.

Valerie Bertinelli

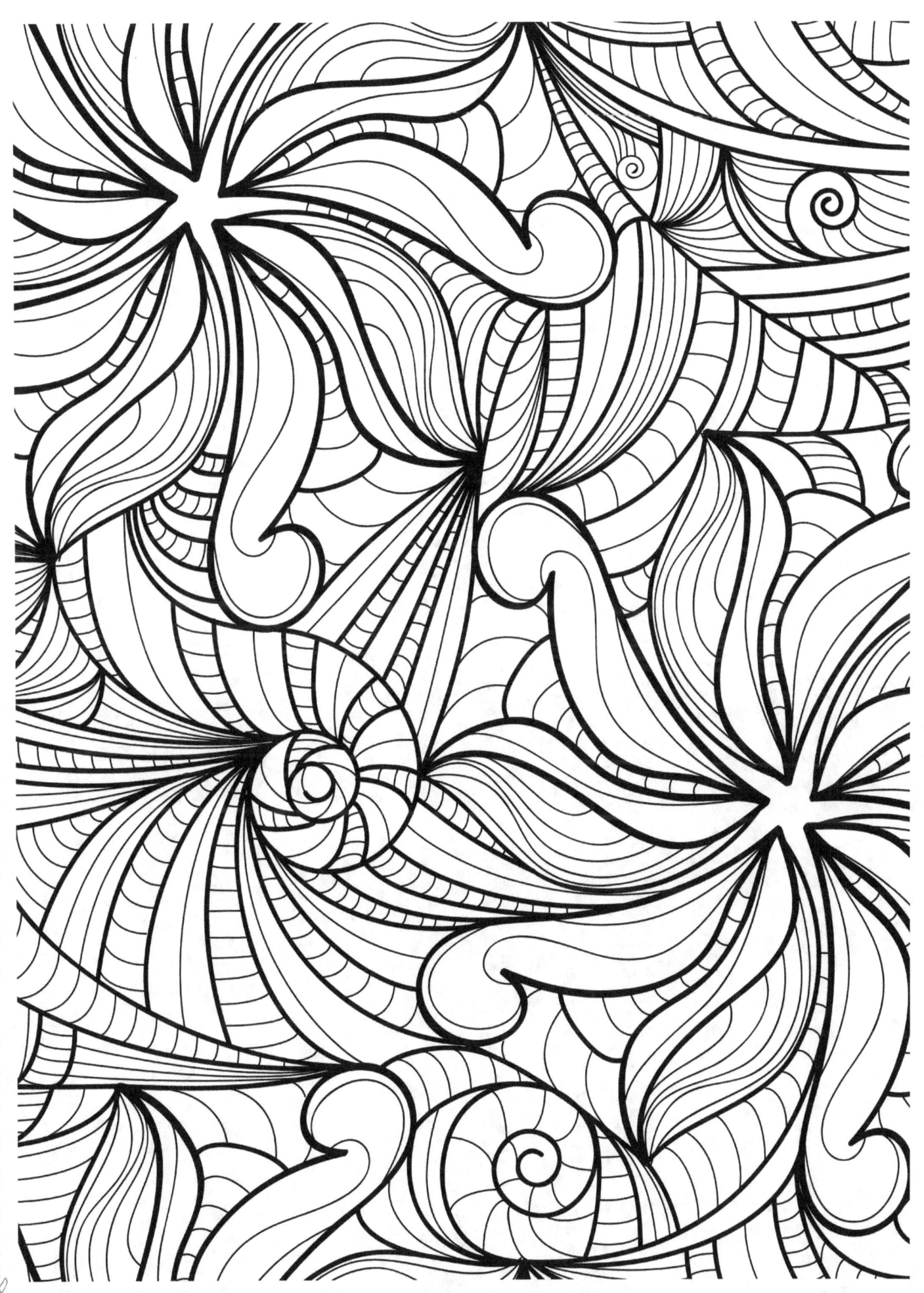

The greatest weapon against stress is our ability to choose one thought over another.

William James

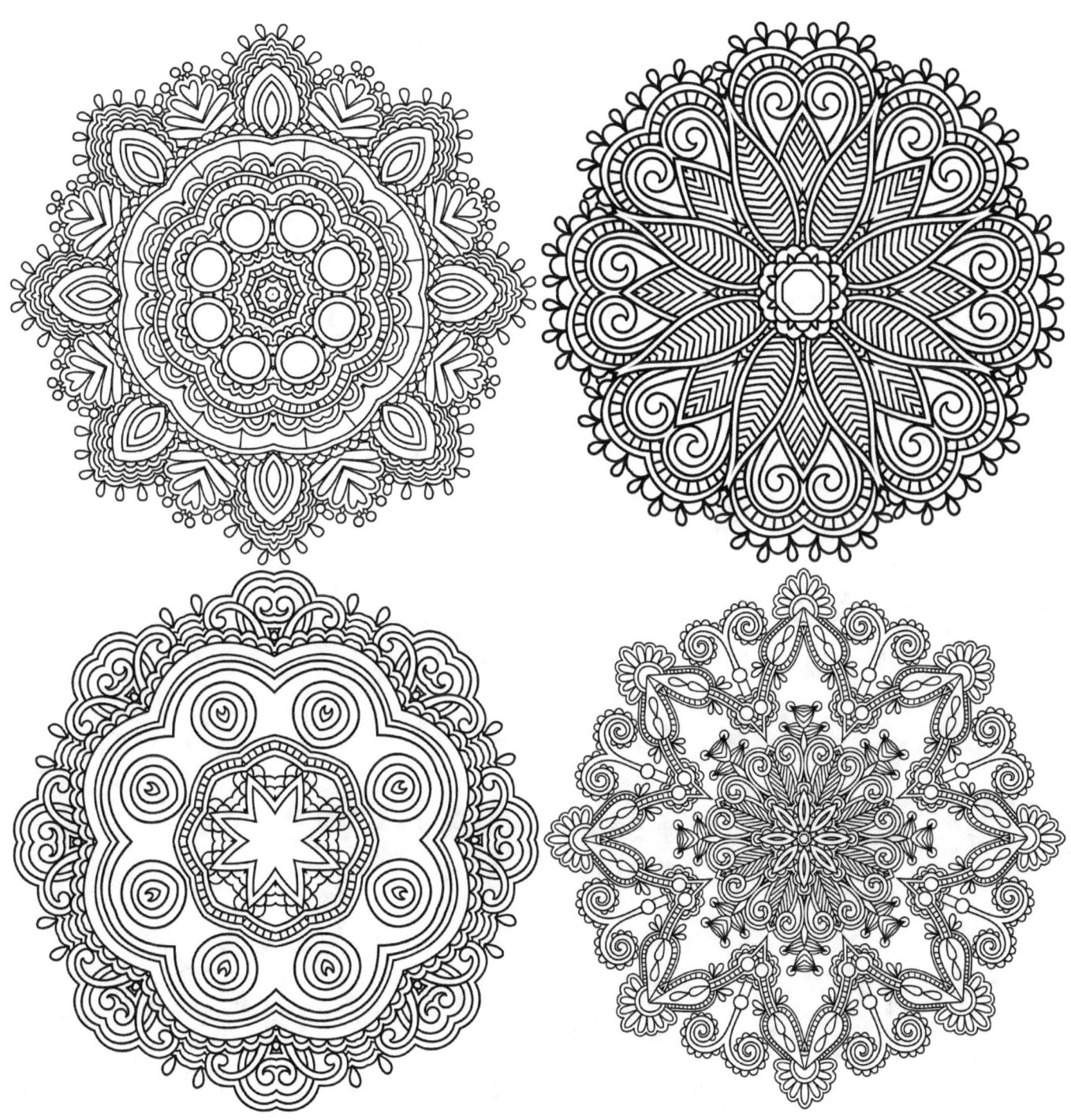

Adopting the right attitude can convert a negative stress into a positive one.

Hans Selye

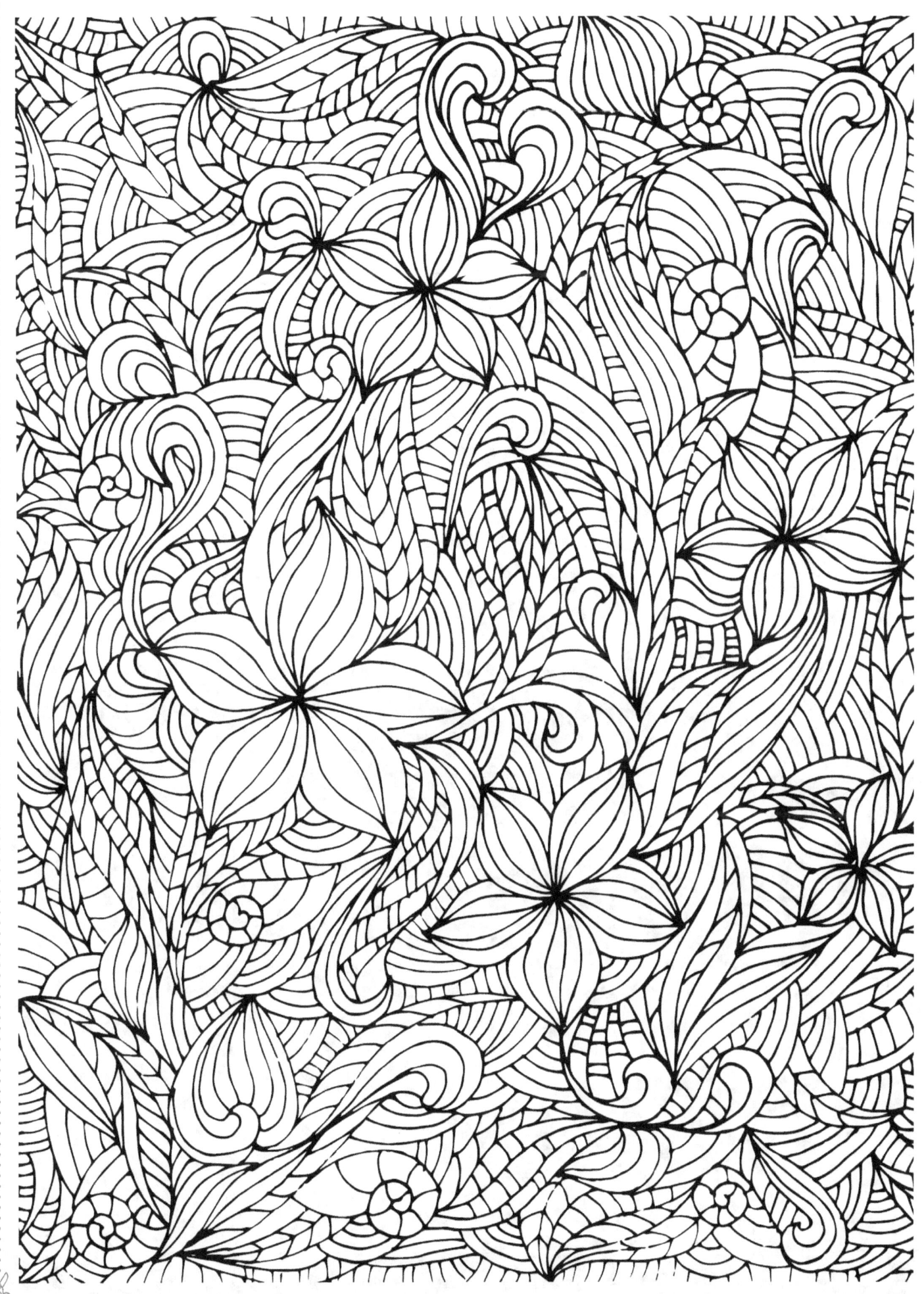

Letting go helps us to live in a more peaceful state of mind and helps restore our balance. It allows others to be responsible for themselves and for us to take our hands off situations that do not belong to us. This frees us from unnecessary stress.

Melody Beattie

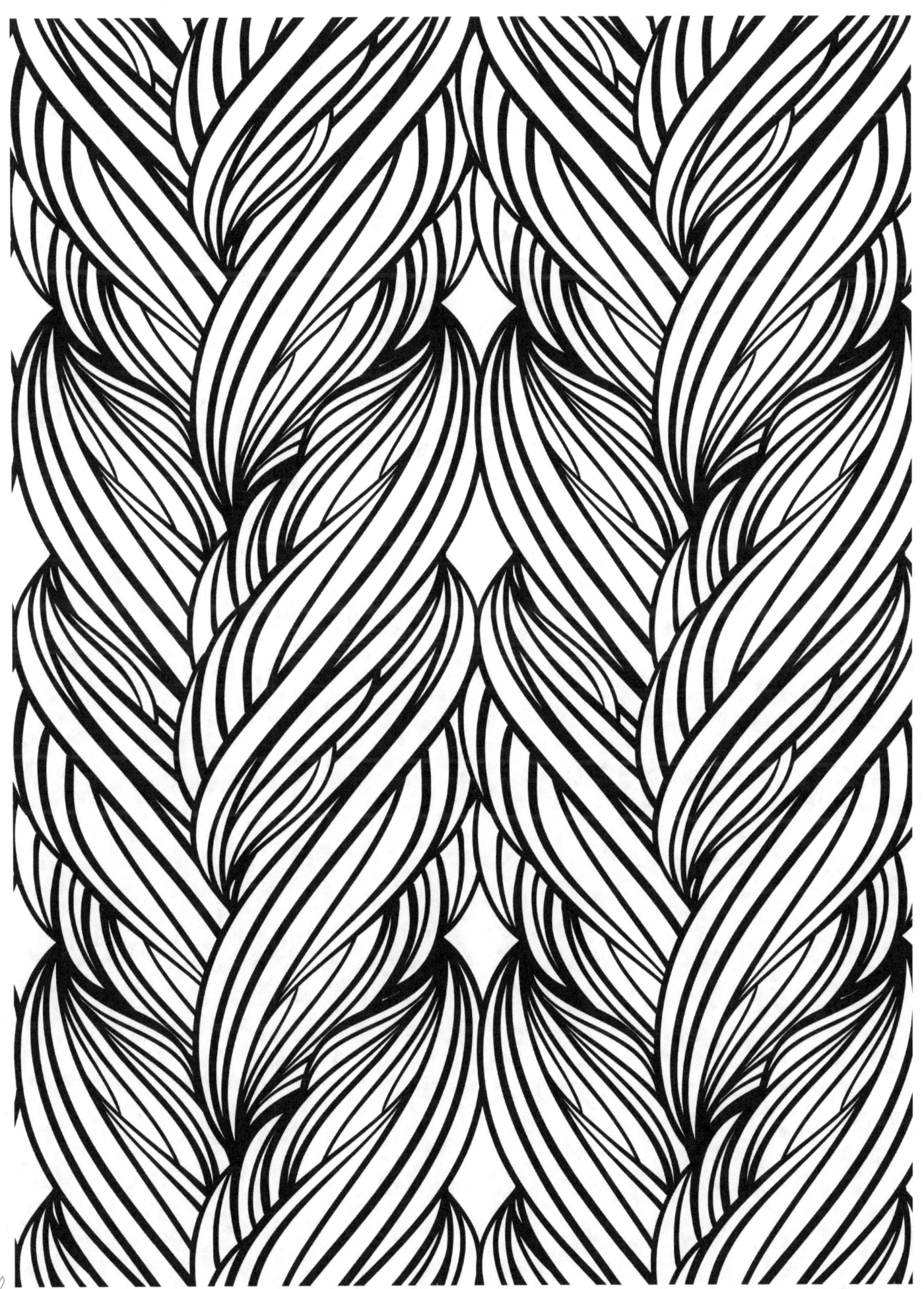

The deepest fear we have, 'the fear beneath all fears,' is the fear of not measuring up, the fear of judgment. It's this fear that creates the stress and depression of everyday life.

Tullian Tchividjian

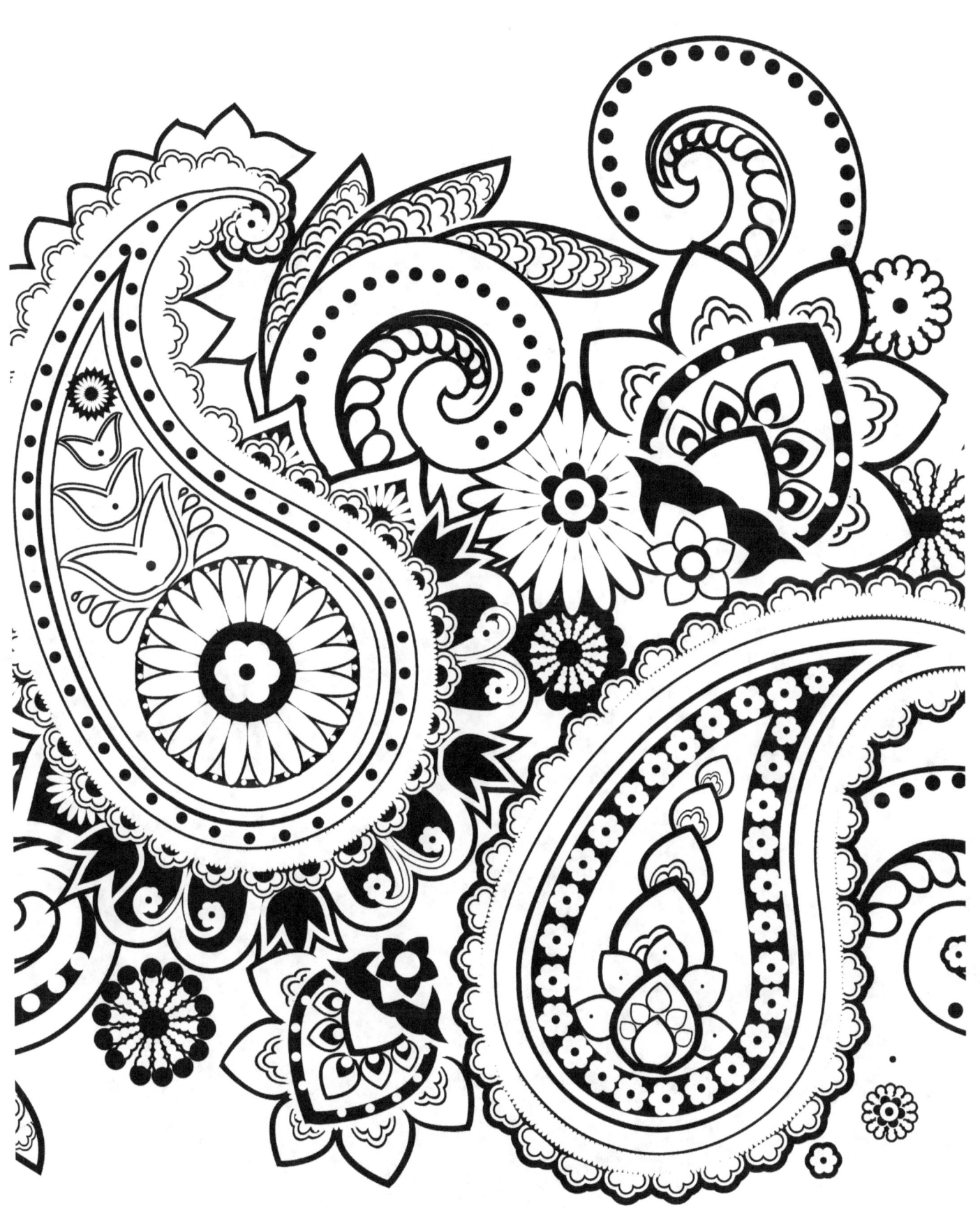

In times of great stress or adversity, it's always best to keep busy, to plow your anger and your energy into something positive.

Lee Iacocca

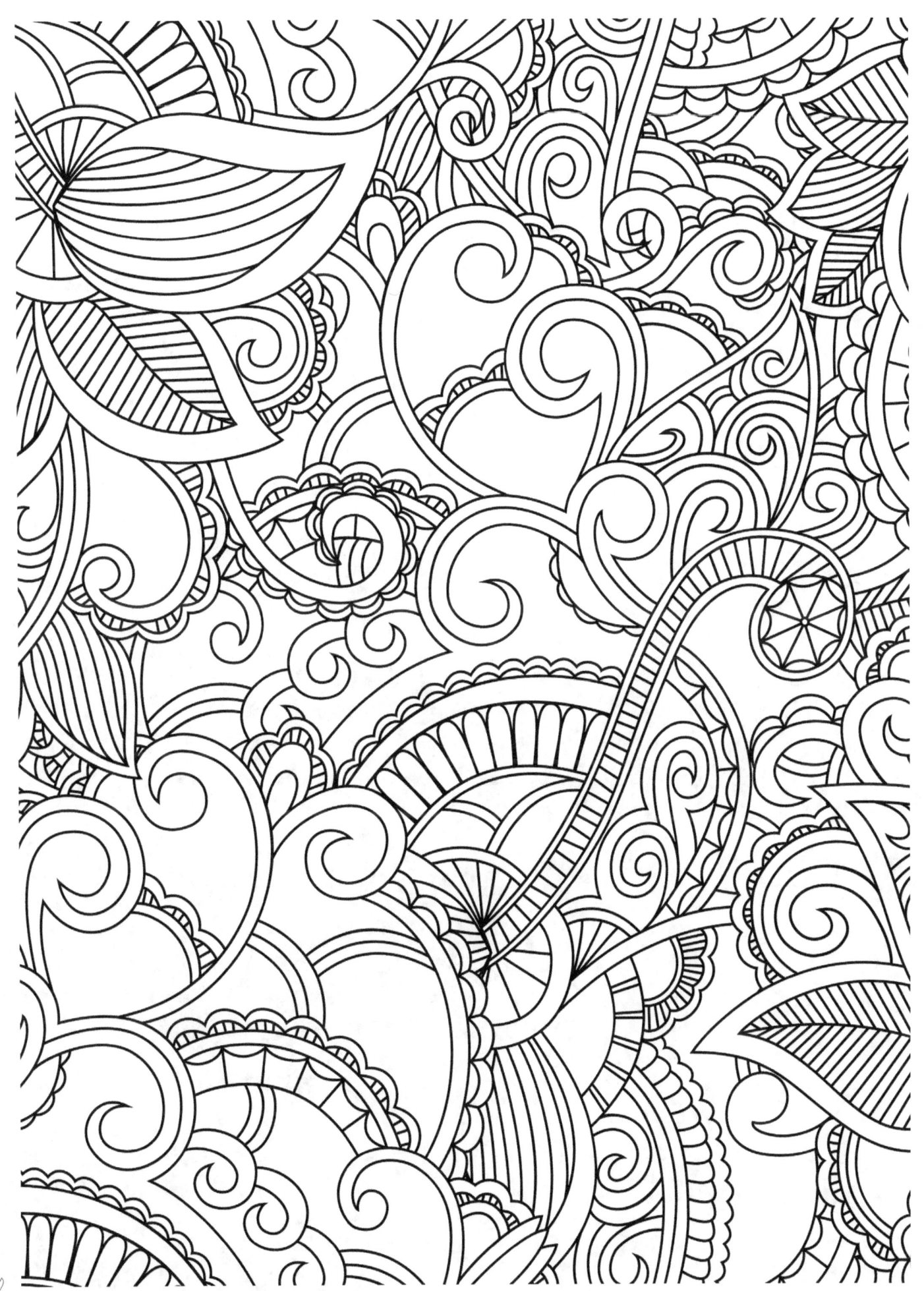

One of the best pieces of advice I ever got was from a horse master. He told me to go slow to go fast. I think that applies to everything in life. We live as though there aren't enough hours in the day but if we do each thing calmly and carefully we will get it done quicker and with much less stress.

Viggo Mortensen

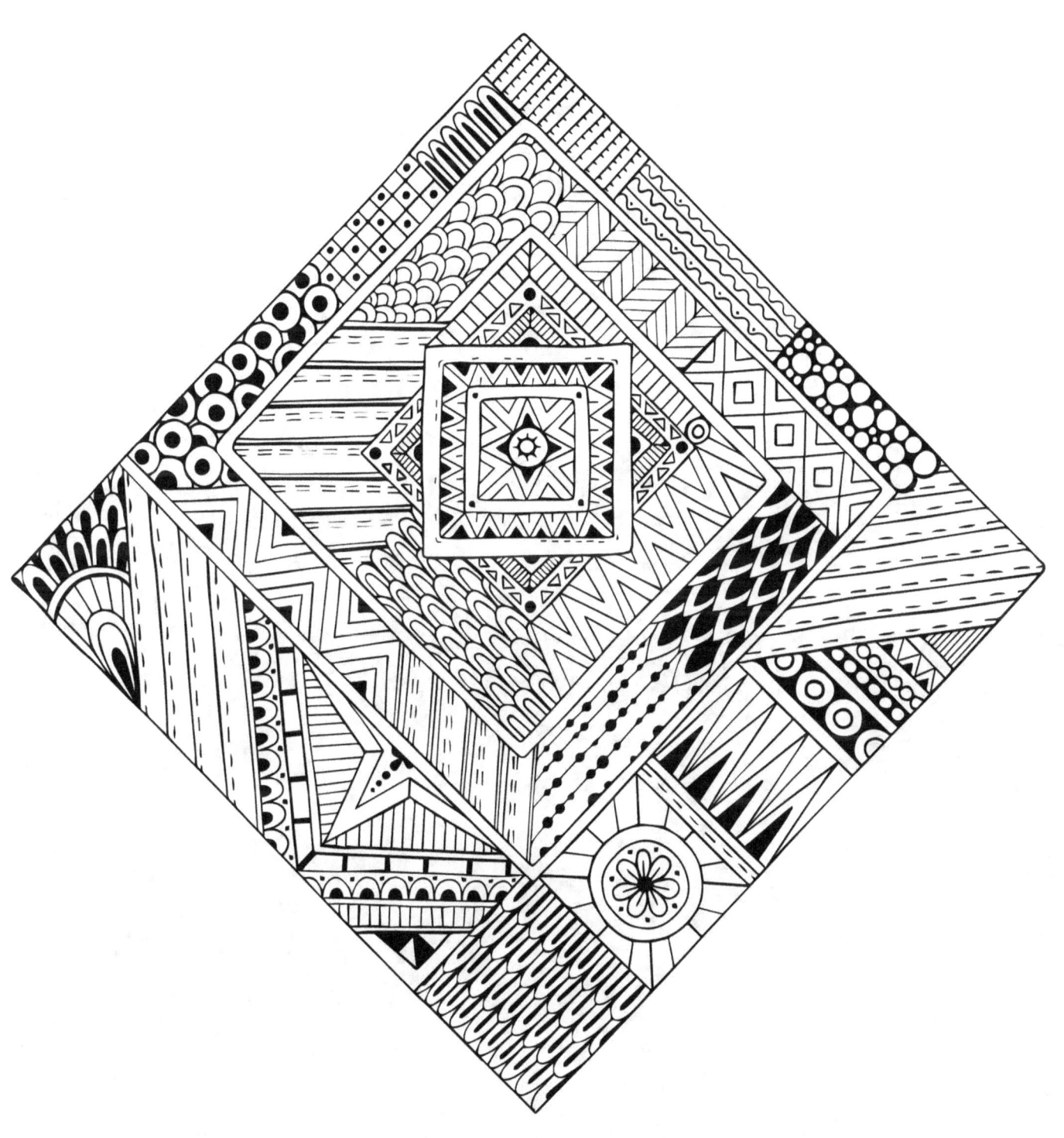

Sometimes when people are under stress, they hate to think, and it's the time when they most need to think.

William J. Clinton

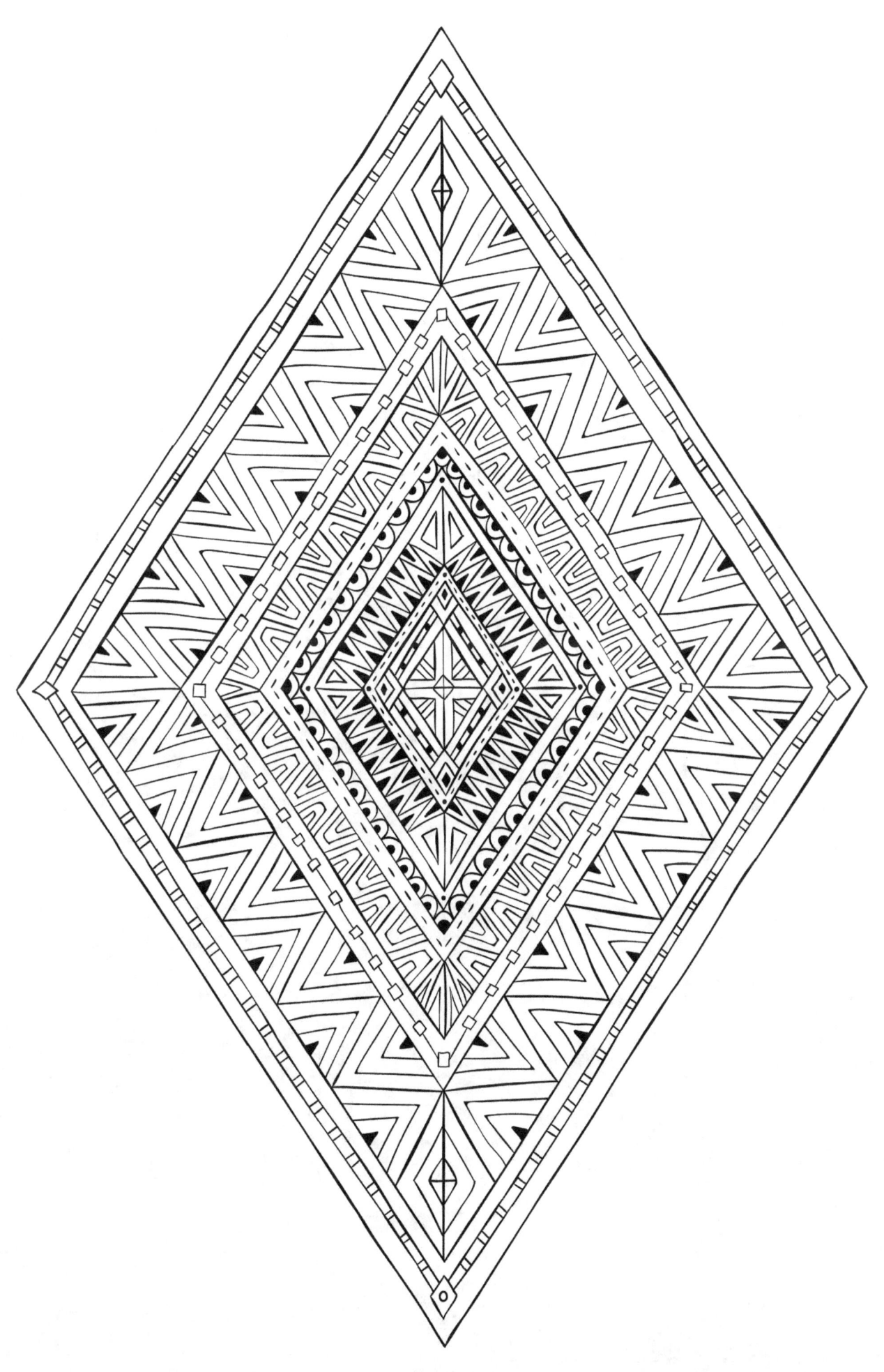

I am an old man and have known a great many troubles, but most of them never happened.

Mark Twain

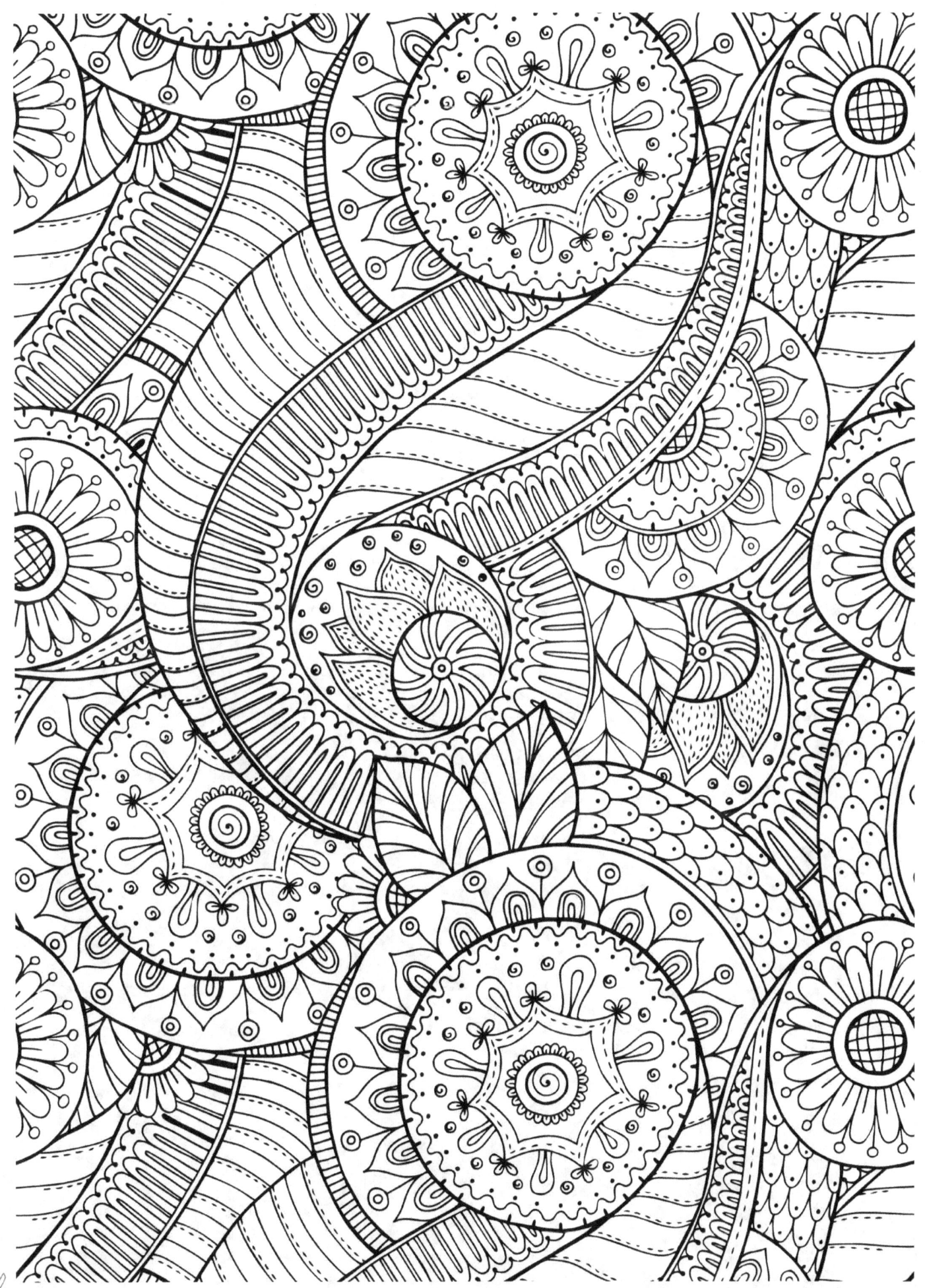

A lot of emotional stress that people go through, some people figure out a way to handle it. They have a strong enough support system to keep going and keep moving forward. And some people, they feel like they don't have that outlet.

Terrell Owens

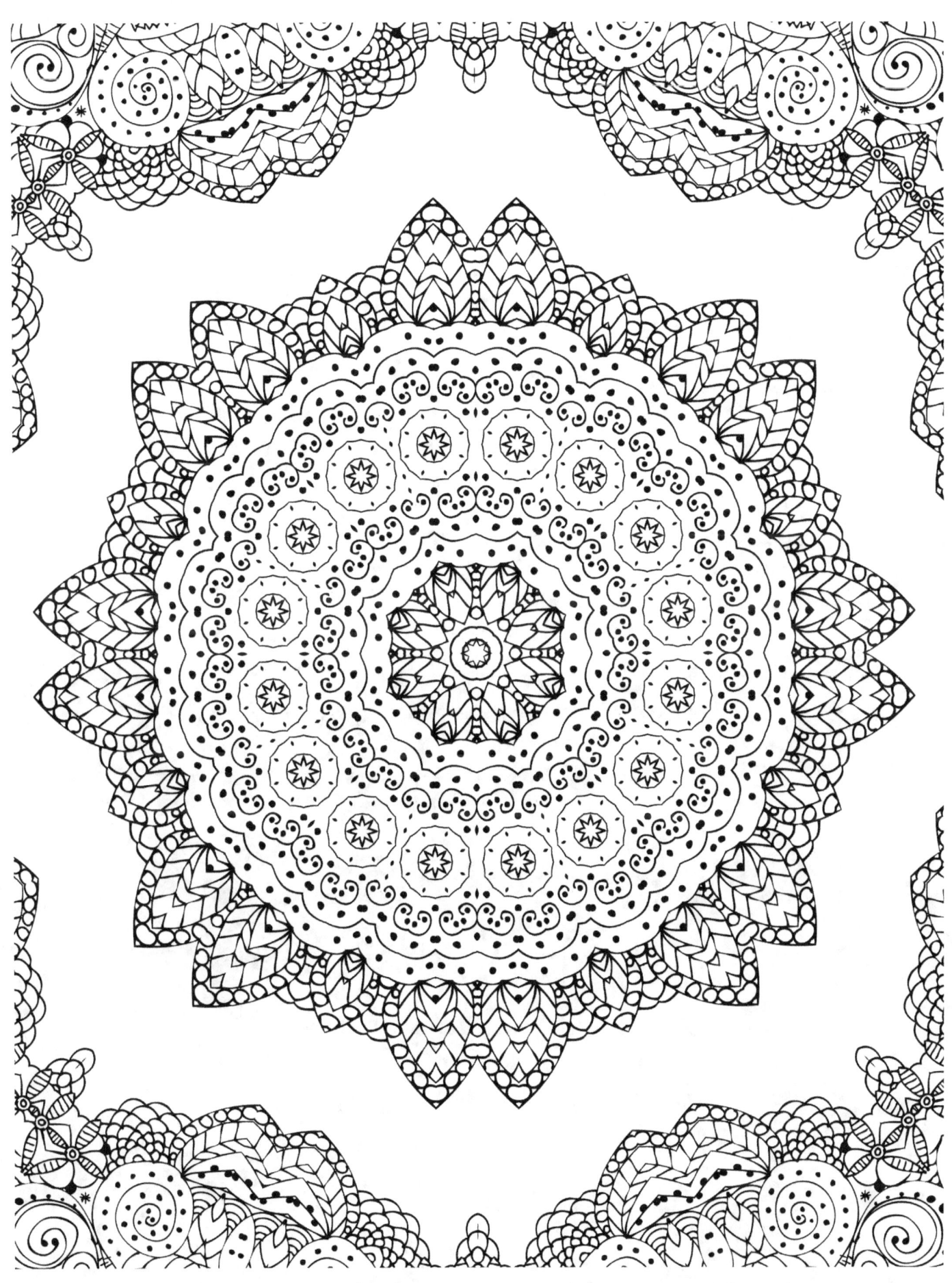

All the suffering, stress, and addiction comes from not realizing you already are what you are looking for.

Jon Kabat-Zinn

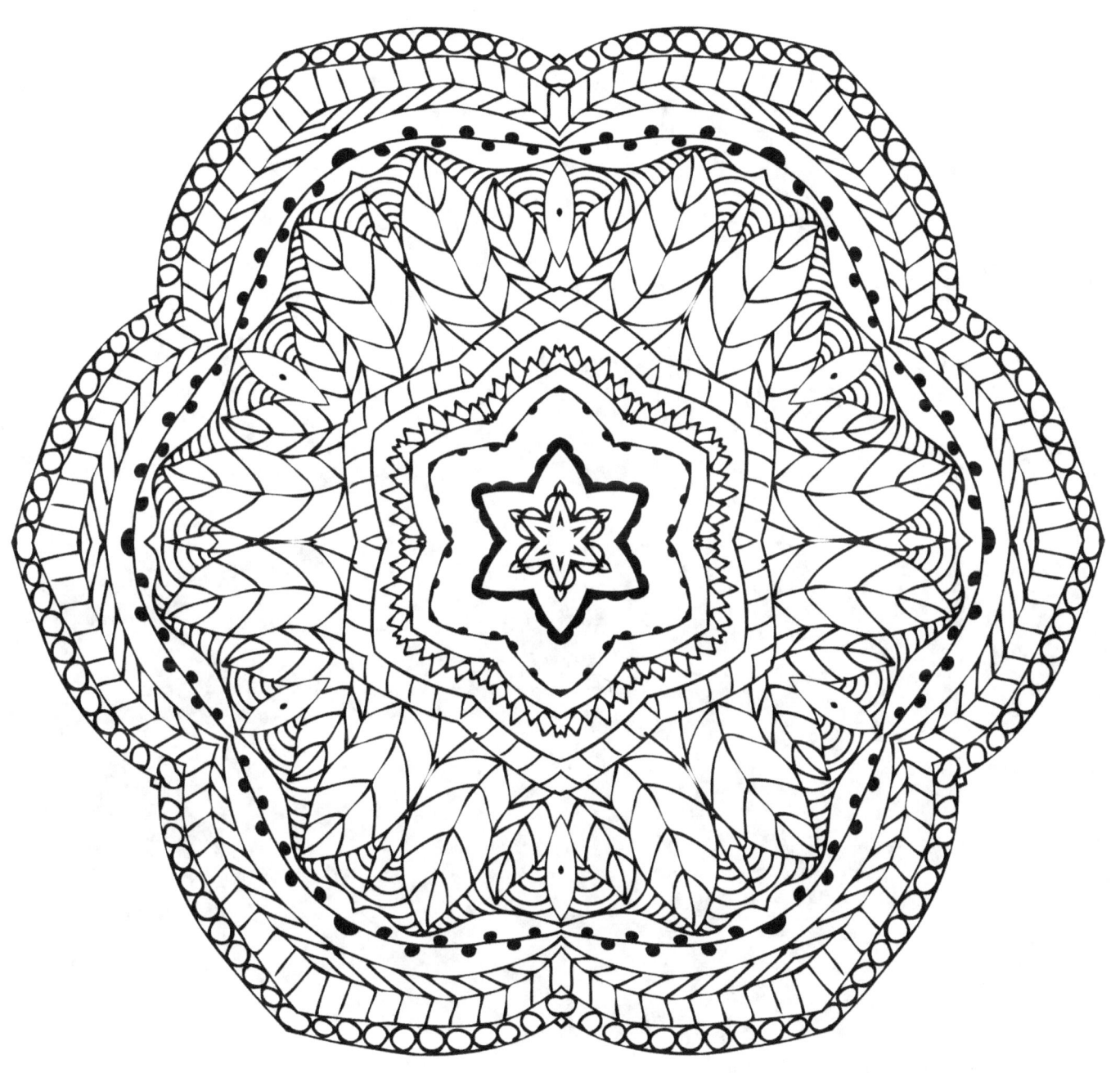

In spite of everything I shall rise again: I will take up my pencil, which I have forsaken in my great discouragement, and I will go on with my drawing.

Valerie Bertinelli

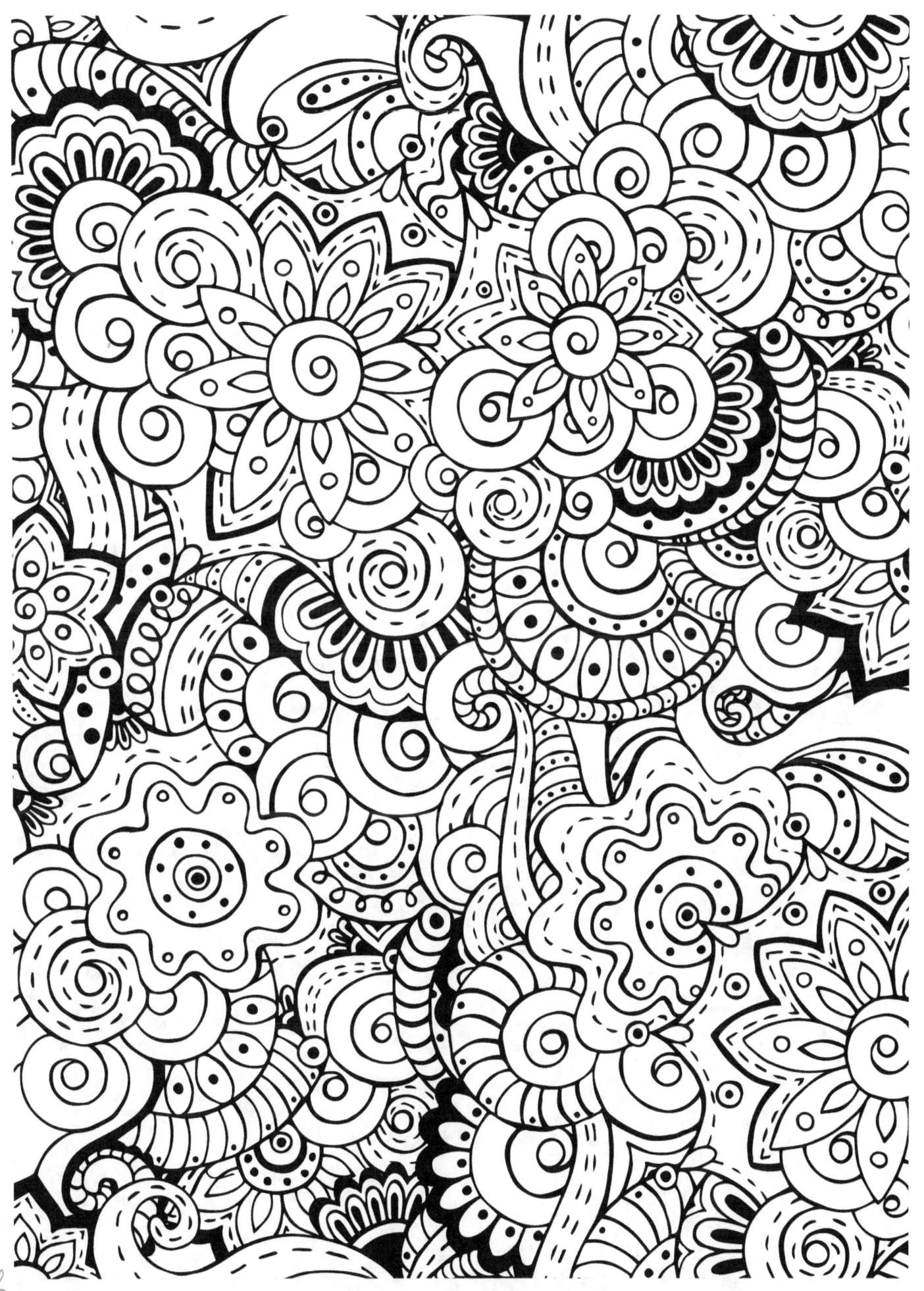

You need to be able to manage stress because hard times will come, and a positive outlook is what gets you through.

Marie Osmond

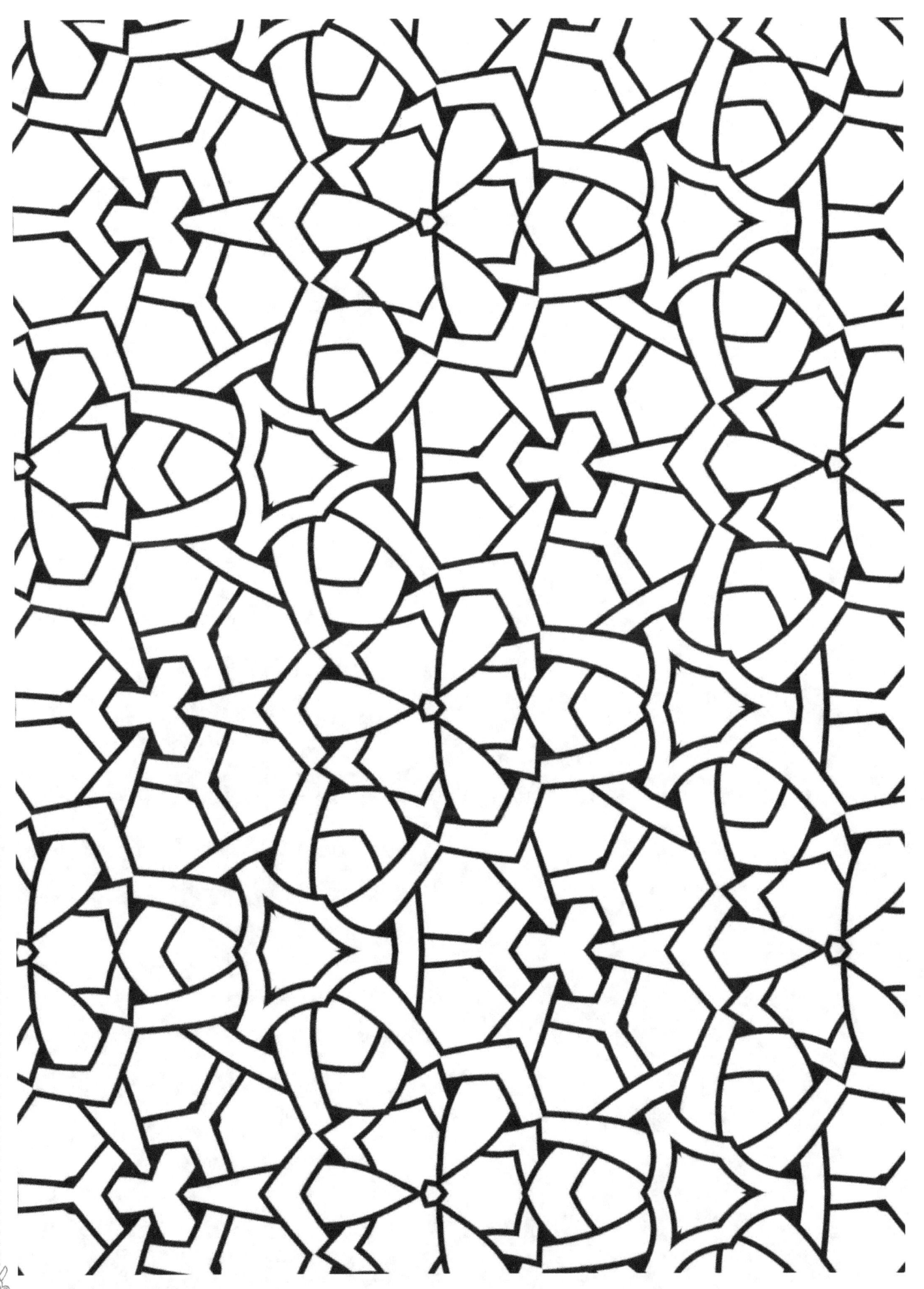

To be a champion, you have to learn to handle stress and pressure. But if you've prepared mentally and physically, you don't have to worry.

Harvey Mackay

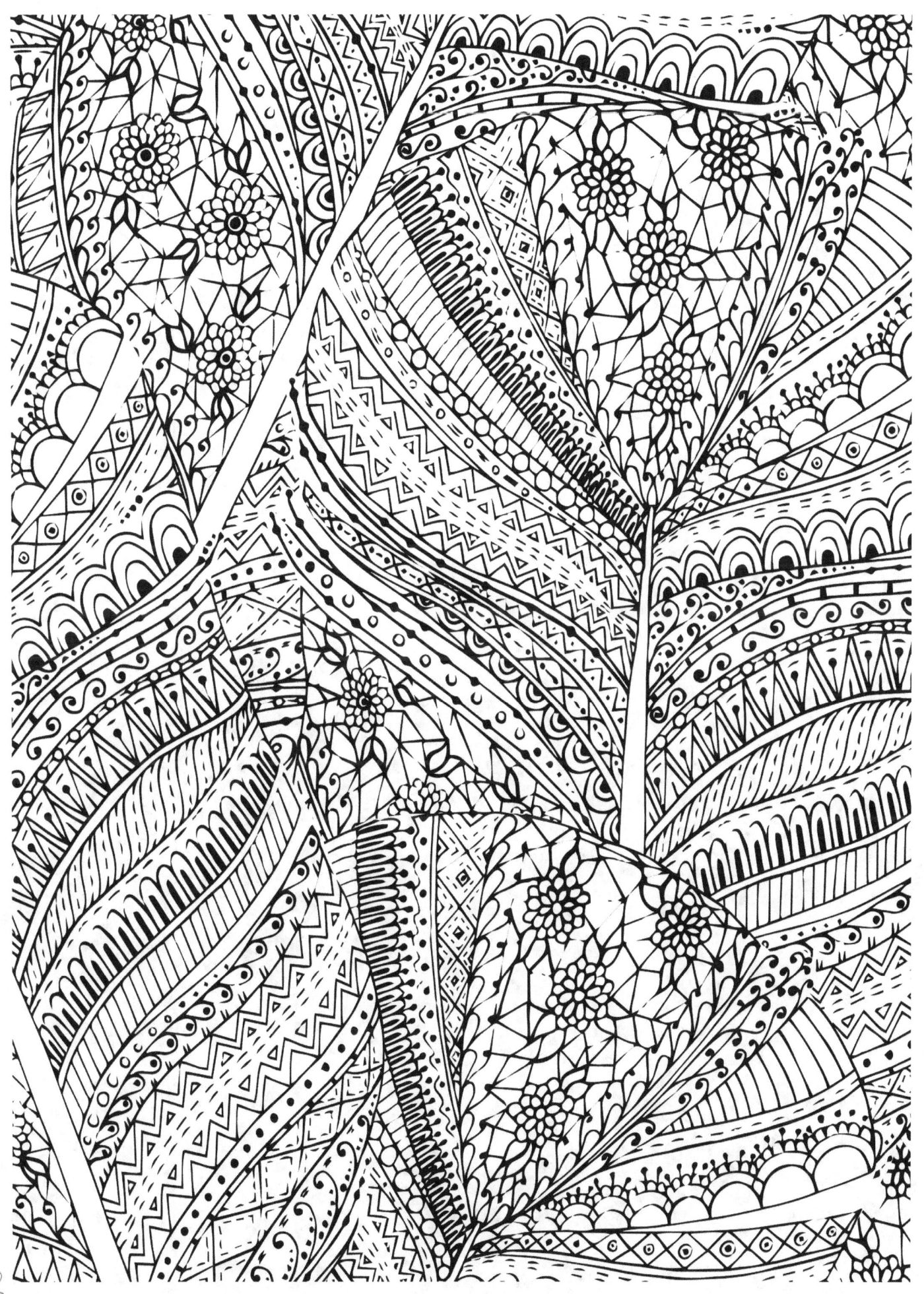

Whenever we feel stressed out, that's a signal that our brain is pumping out stress hormones. If sustained over months and years, those hormones can ruin our health and make us a nervous wreck.

Daniel Goleman

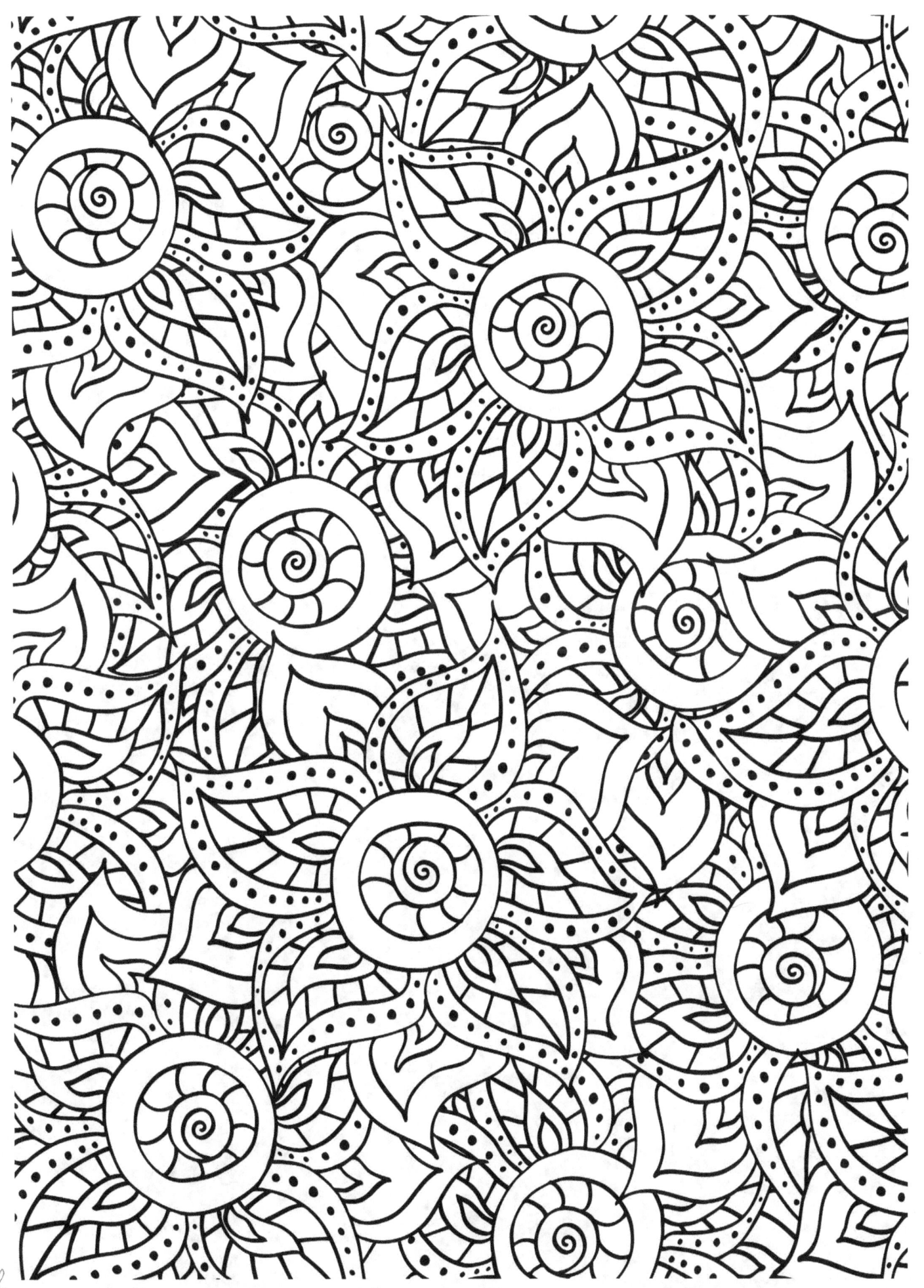

Getting stress out of your life takes more than prayer alone. You must take action to make changes and stop doing whatever is causing the stress. You can learn to calm down in the way you handle things.

Joyce Meyer

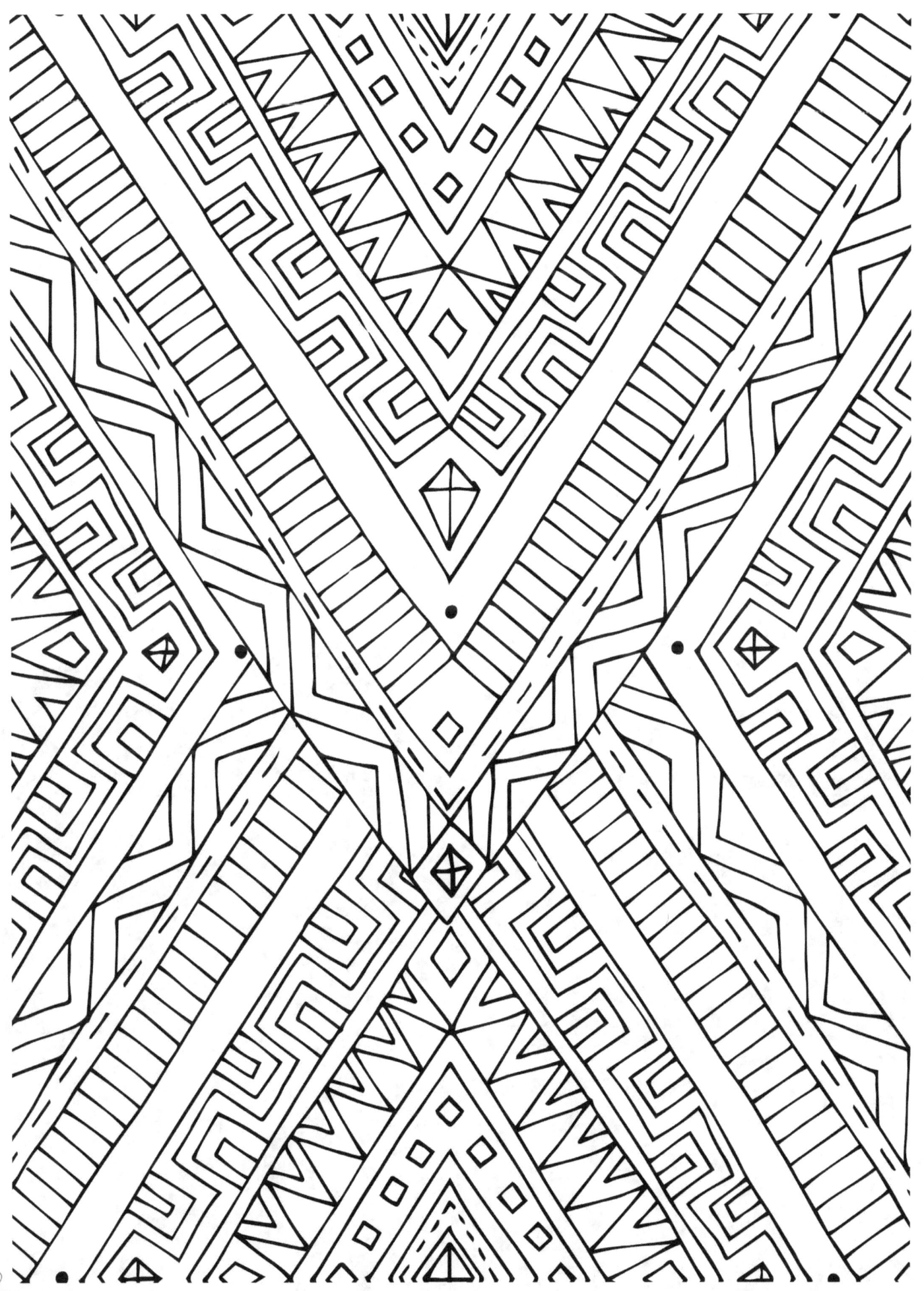

If you ask what is the single most important key to longevity, I would have to say it is avoiding worry, stress and tension. And if you didn't ask me, I'd still have to say it.

George Burns

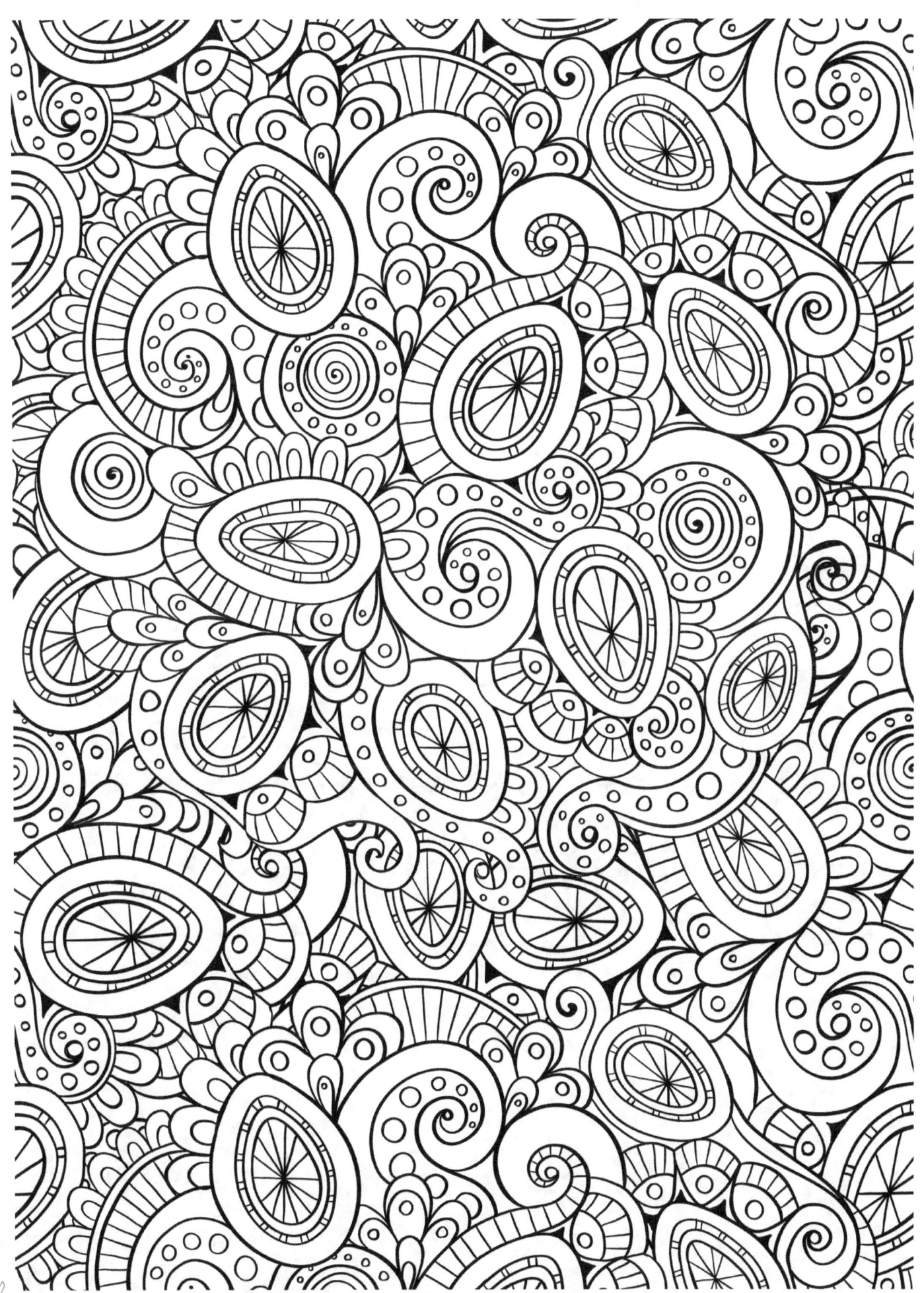

Many of us feel stress and get overwhelmed not because we're taking on too much, but because we're taking on too little of what really strengthens us.

Marcus Buckingham

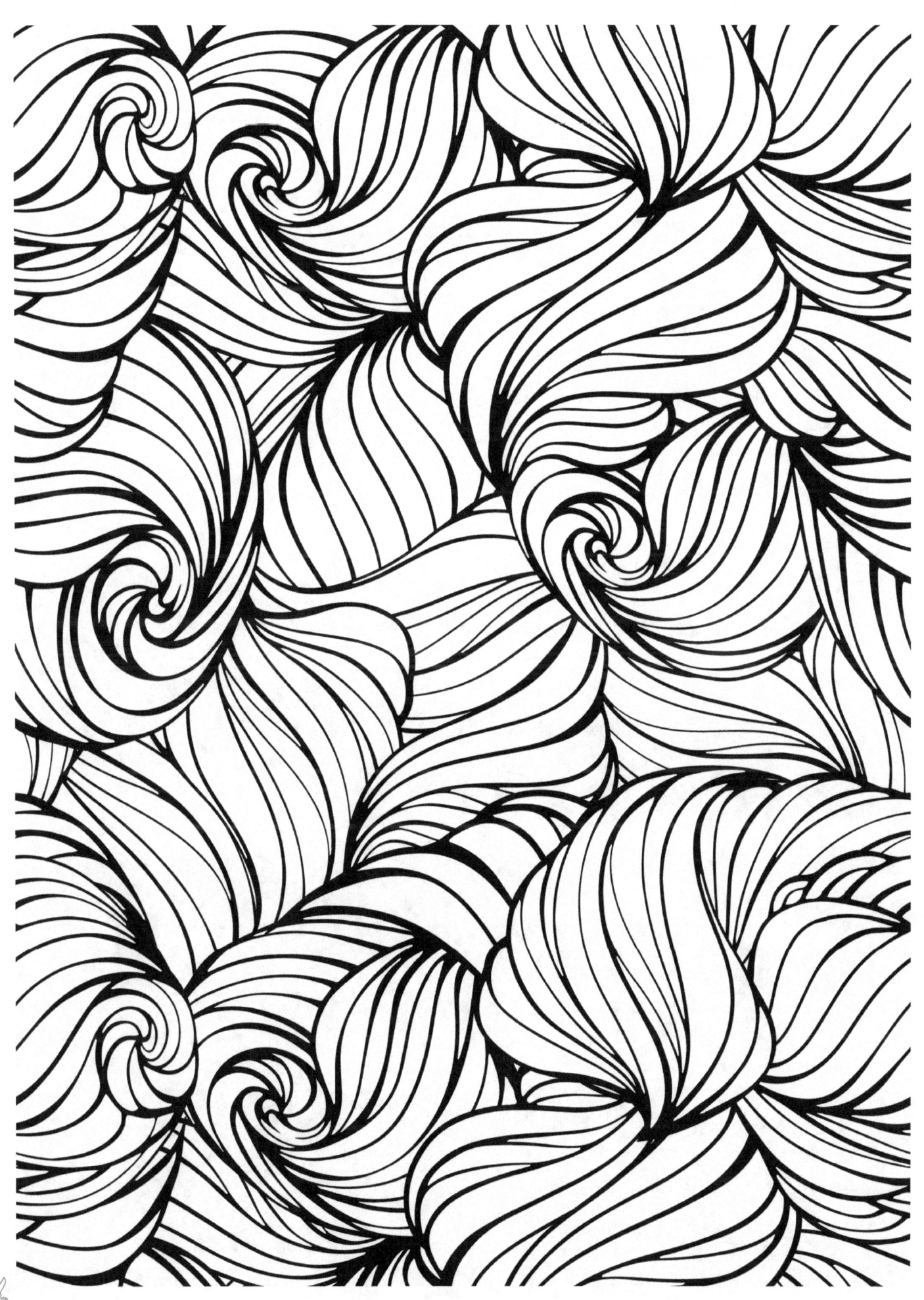

Every stress leaves an indelible scar, and the organism pays for its survival after a stressful situation by becoming a little older.

Hans Selye

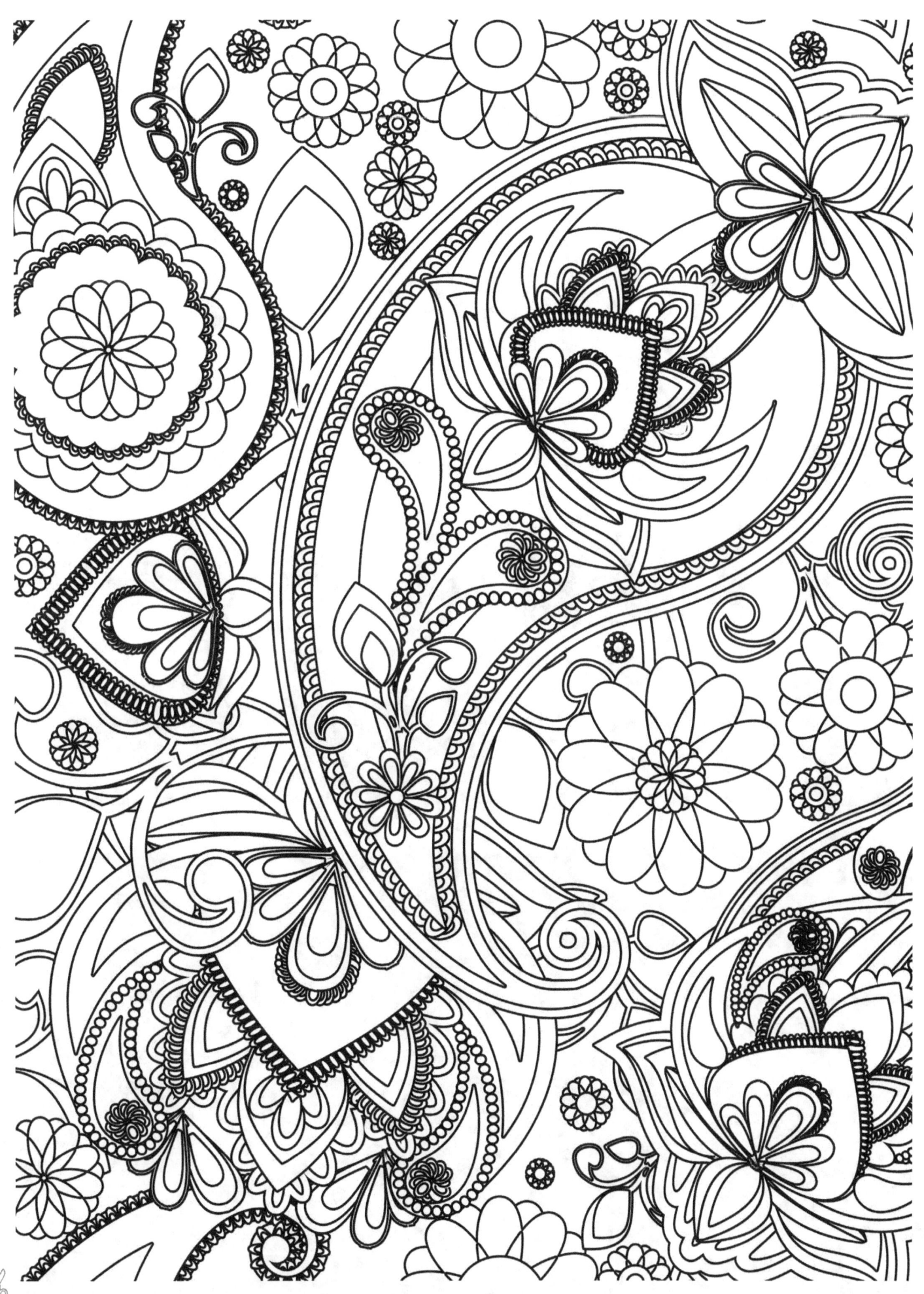

The components of anxiety, stress, fear, and anger do not exist independently of you in the world. They simply do not exist in the physical world, even though we talk about them as if they do.

Wayne Dyer

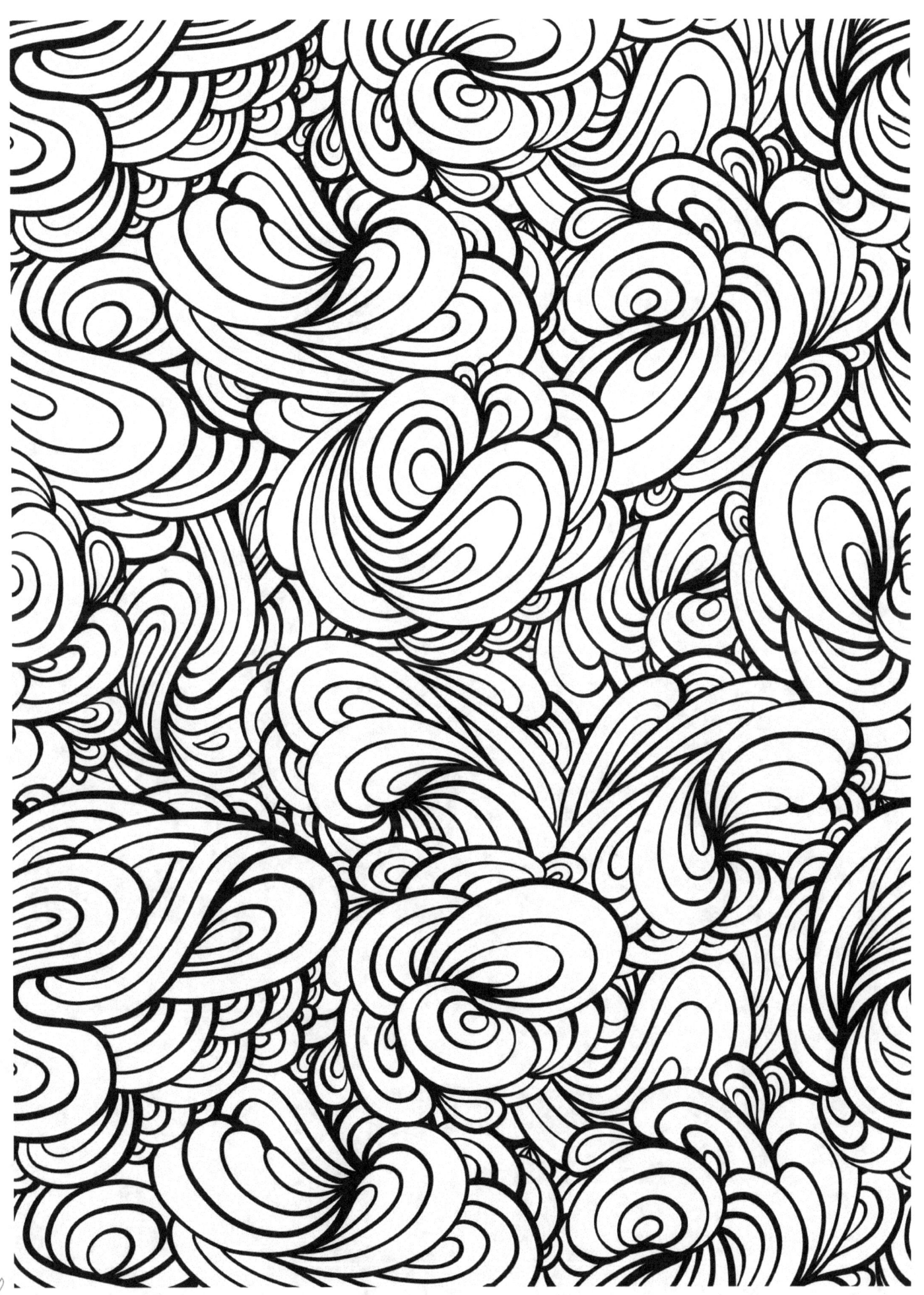

The life of inner peace, being harmonious and without stress, is the easiest type of existence.

Norman Vincent Peale

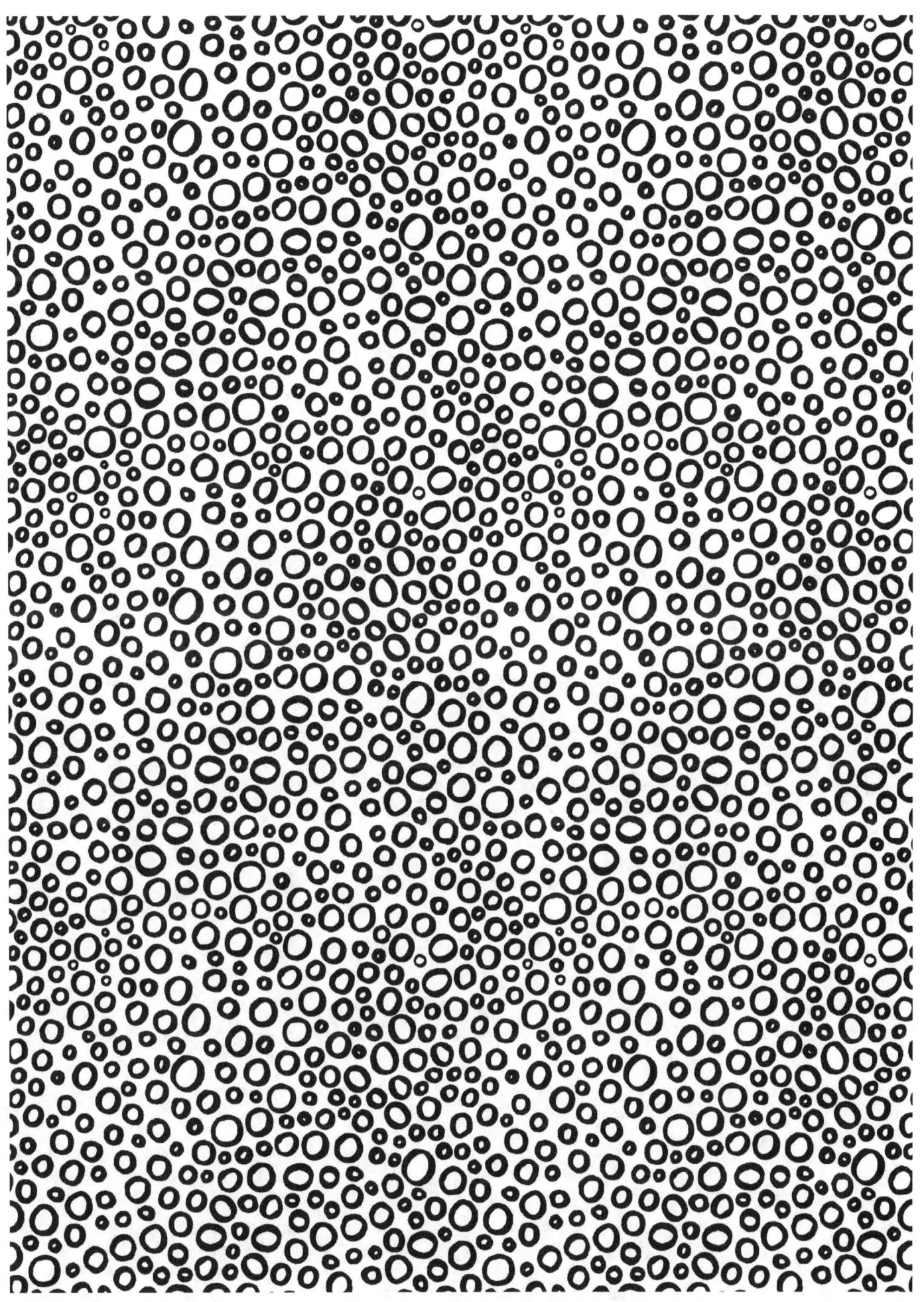

Once you accept, truly accept, that stuff will happen to you and there is nothing you can do about it, stress miraculously leaves your life.

Srikumar Rao

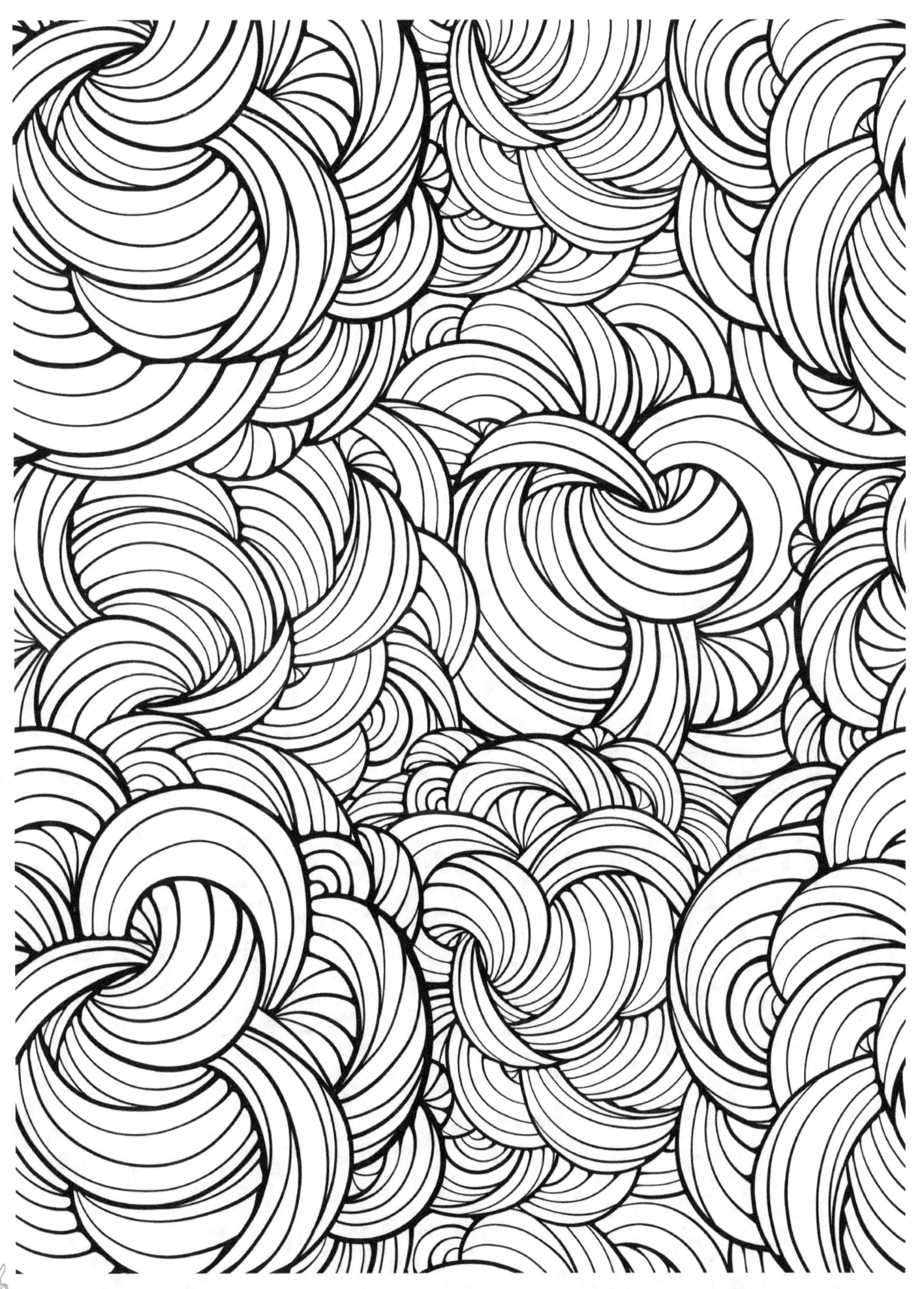

Stress is an important dragon to slay - or at least tame - in your life.

Marilu Henner

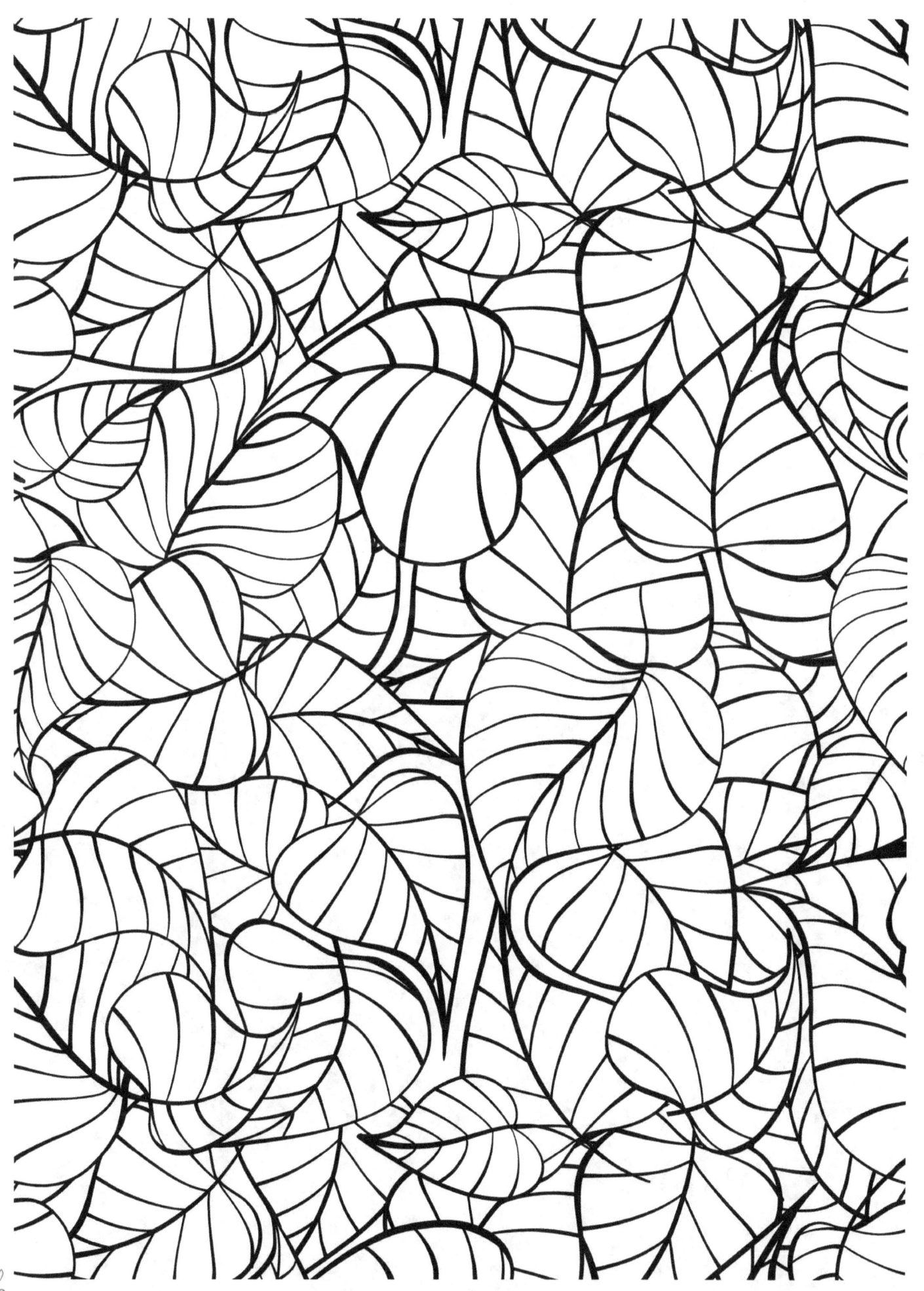

I'm free of stress and worries now because if I don't like something I'm doing, I just find the fun in it instead of being miserable.

Jenny McCarthy

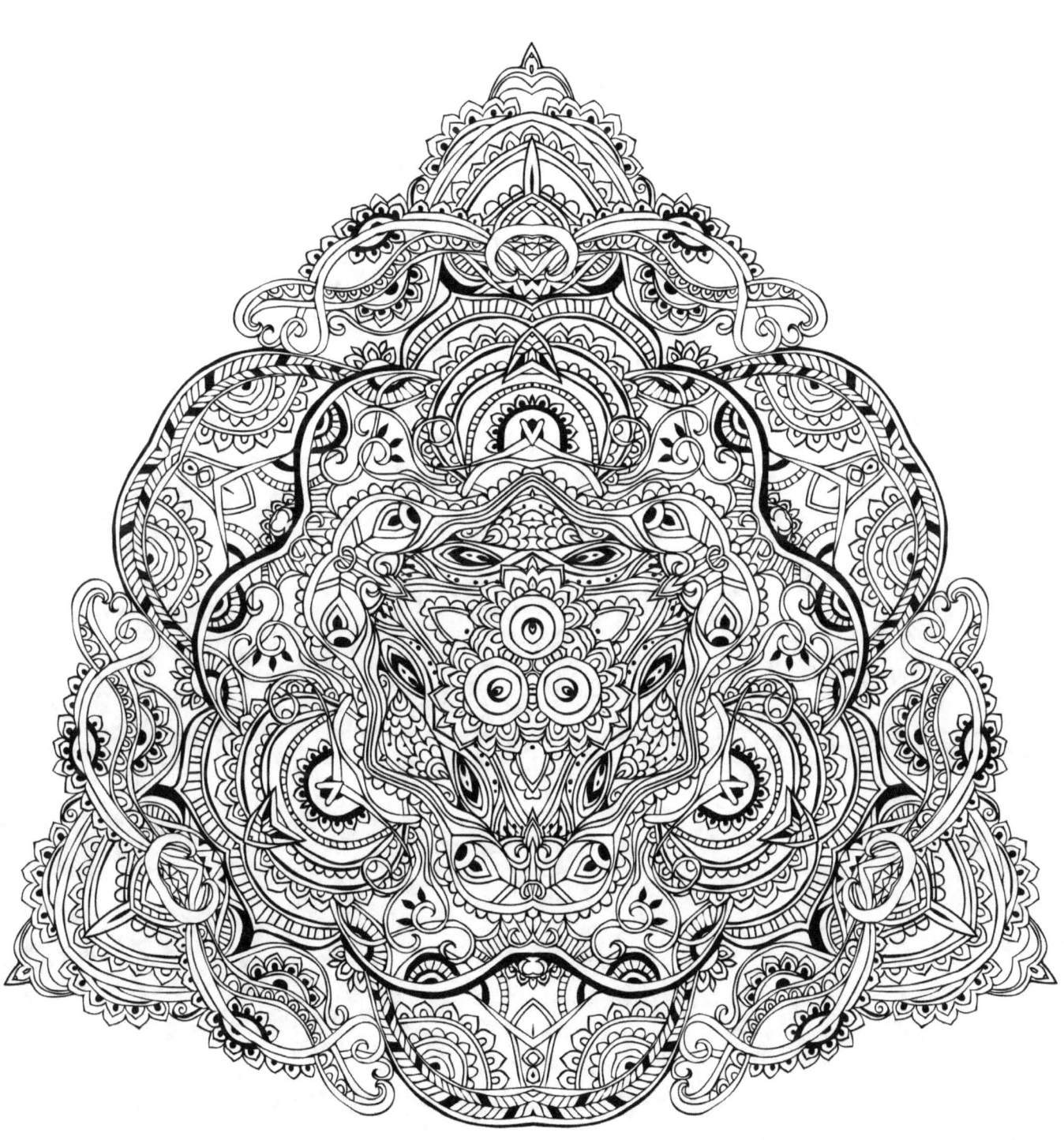

Live in the moment, day by day, and don't stress about the future. People are so caught up in looking into the future, that they kind of lose what's in front of them.

Jenna Ushkowitz

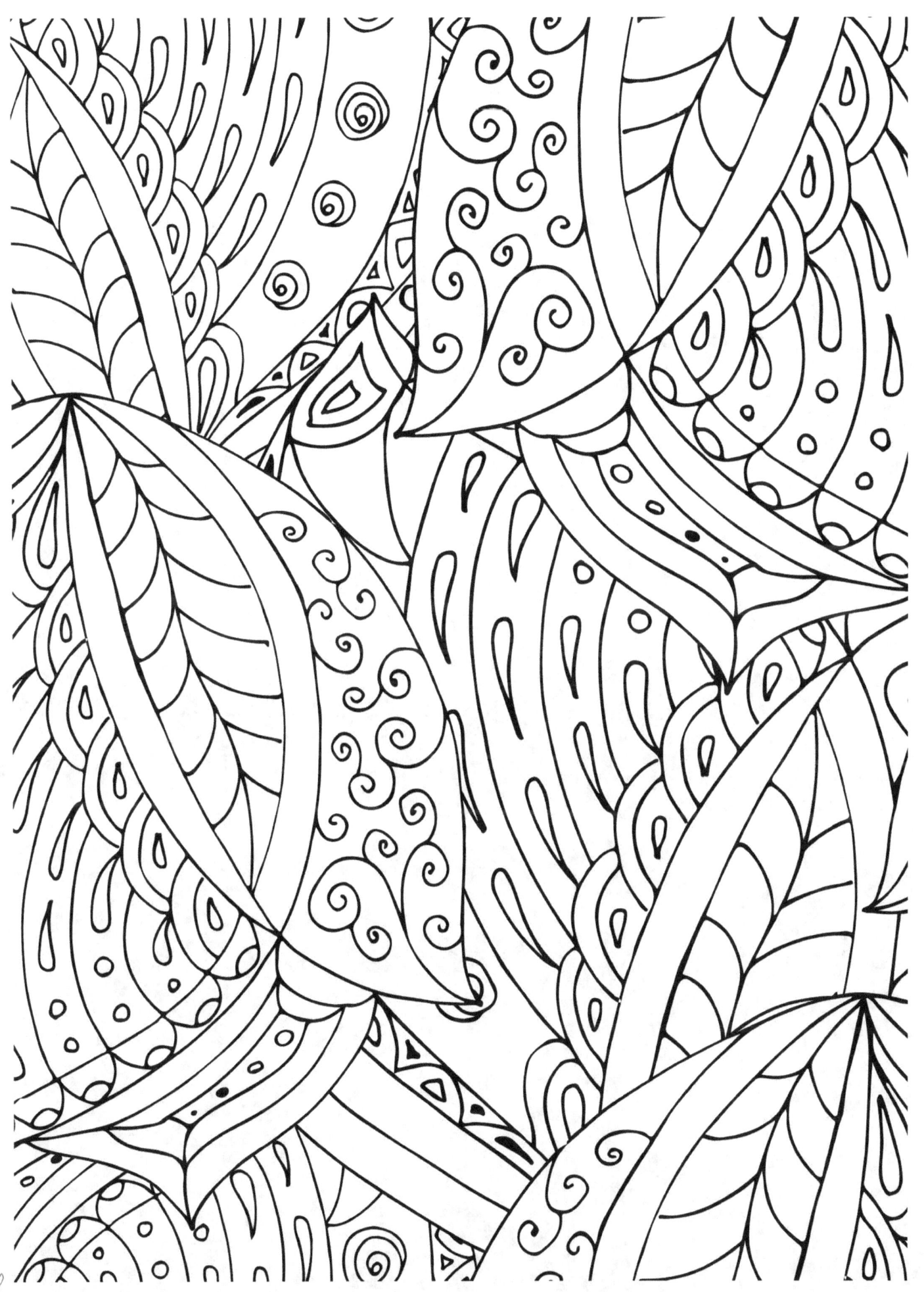

Stress is basically a disconnection from the earth, a forgetting of the breath. Stress is an ignorant state. It believes that everything is an emergency. Nothing is that important. Just lie down.

Natalie Goldberg

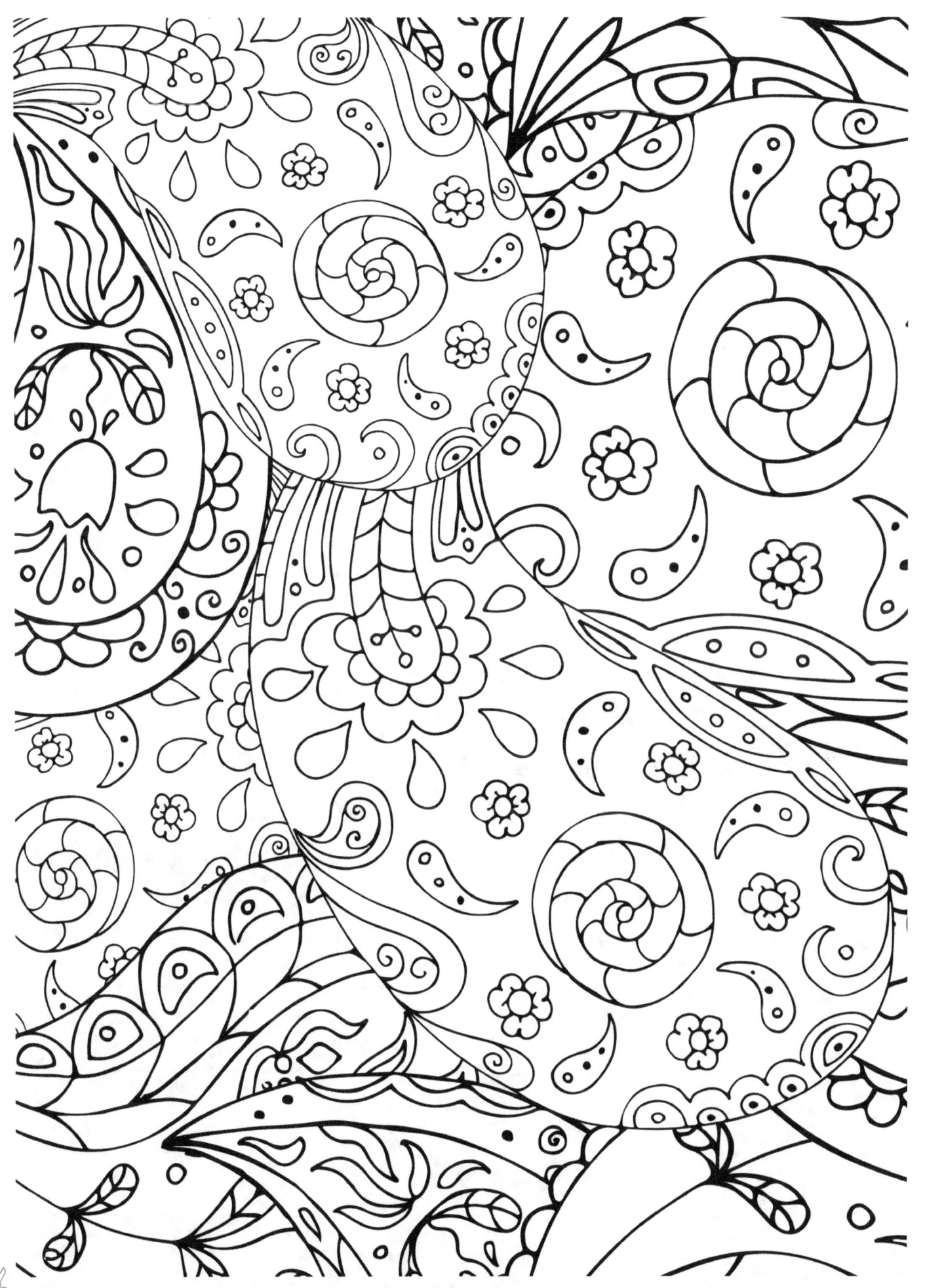

It takes a real storm in the average person's life to make him realize how much worrying he has done over the squalls.

Author Unknown

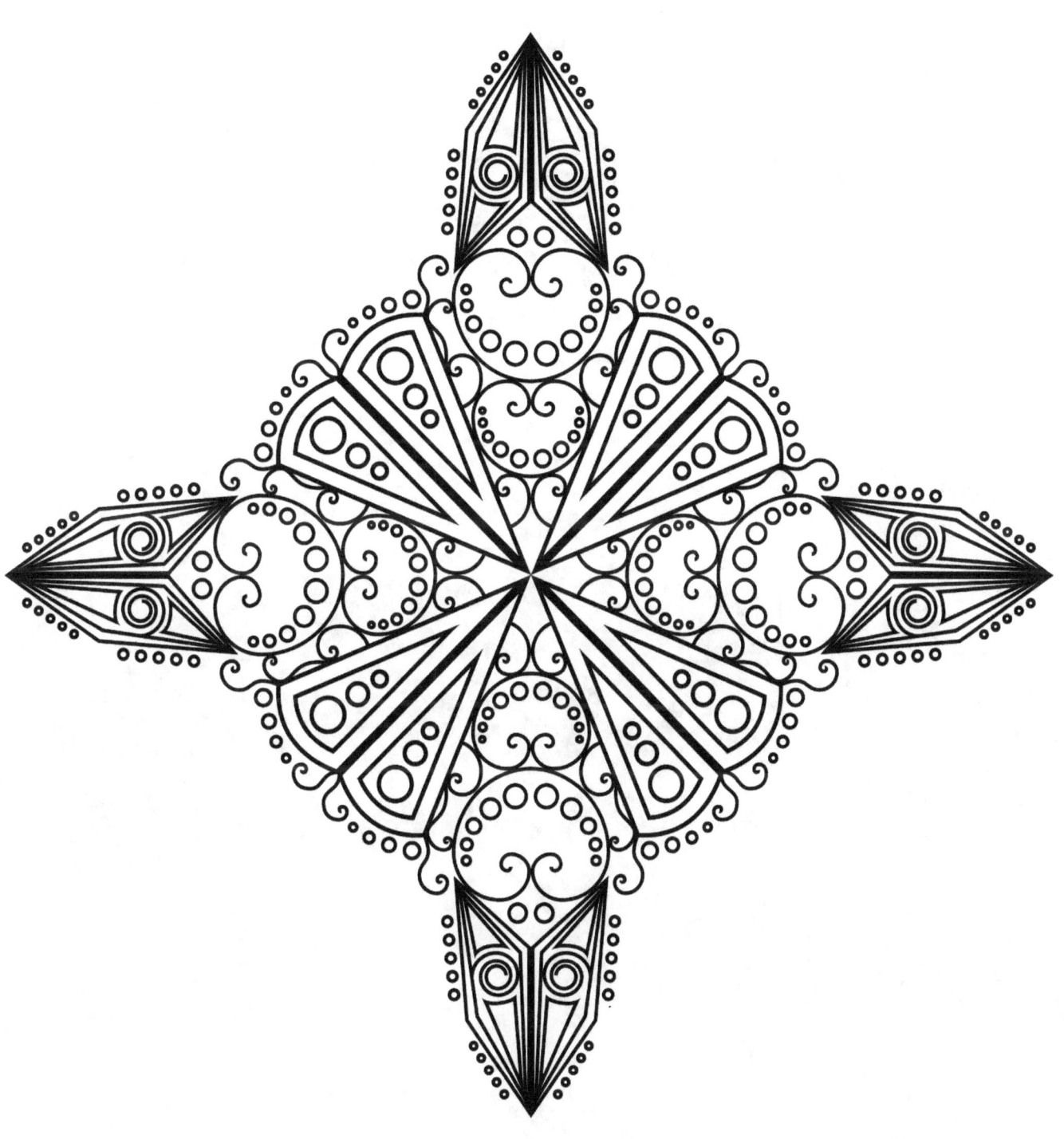